INTRODUCTION TO CONTEMPORARY INDIGENOUS HOUSING

OTHER BOOKS BY NORBERT SCHOENAUER

With Stanley Seeman. *The Court-Garden House.*
Montreal: McGill-Queen's University Press, 1962.

With John Bland. *University Housing in Canada.*
Montreal: McGill-Queen's University Press, 1966.

Architecture Montreal. Montreal:
The Province of Quebec Association of Architects, 1967.

Collective and Conjunctive Habitation. In Preparation.

INTRODUCTION TO CONTEMPORARY INDIGENOUS HOUSING
by Norbert Schoenauer

with illustrations by
George Juhasz and Norbert Schoenauer

published by
REPORTER BOOKS
Montreal, 1973

Typesetting and design by Academic, Professional
and Scholarly Publishing Services, Montreal

Printed and bound in Canada.

To my students
who unknowingly taught me

PREFACE

This manuscript represents the first part of a course entitled "History of Housing", offered by the author at the School of Architecture, McGill University. Its content is limited to non-urban contemporary indigenous housing. Urban housing constitutes the second half of the course and is yet to be edited for publication.

Vernacular and anonymous architecture, of course, has been studied by many architects, anthropologists, geographers and adventurous travellers. Some architects have analysed and compared its structures, others its forms and the materials used as well as the ingenuous and even ingenious way in which these buildings meet climatic requirements, but few have viewed them as entire examples of architectural response to cultural and physical forces. The author has therefore no illusion that the subject material of this manuscript is novel; on the contrary, it is well known. But, sometimes looking again at what is familiar, one sees things one has not seen before.

ACKNOWLEDGEMENTS

The author is indebted:

—to Miss Maureen Anderson for editing and giving constructive criticism;

—to Miss Christine Cote for typing the manuscript;

—to Mr. George Juhasz for preparation of perspective illustrations;

—to Mr. Darrell Dickie for editing for press;

—to "National Geographic" for giving me insight into the habitats of various societies
and bringing, figuratively speaking, the world to my letterbox.

TABLE OF CONTENTS

INTRODUCTION

Basically, indigenous housing is viewed in this study as architectural responses to a set of cultural and physical forces intrinsic to their respective environments. This view has not always been shared, since similarities in building forms belonging to two widely separated simple societies were often attributed to some prehistoric common heritage, cross influences or even to chance or coincidence. In most instances, however, these notions were far removed from reality. A much more realistic and plausible explanation can be found in the theory that similar determinative forces bring about similarities in building form. Naturally, this environmental determinism includes not only the forces of physical and human geography, but also those determinants that derive from the relationships between man and his culture, the latter being the product of physical, social, economic, religious and political forces.

The phenomenon of similarity derived from environmental determinism can be most easily demonstrated by the dwelling forms found in the simplest social organizations such as those of the Australian Aborigines and African Bushmen, both groups inhabiting beehive huts practically indistinguishable from each other and both forms being simple architectural reponses to a few identical causal forces. This identity should not be confused with similarities in building structures found in advanced and literate societies where indeed an exchange of ideas and many cross influences have brought about similar architectural results. Of course, in the absence of cross influences, it must be remembered that the likelihood of identical dwelling forms decreases proportionately with increased complexity of determinant variations.

An emphasis of anthropo-geographic and socio-economic factors suggests the adoption of a primary classification similar to that of Gabriele Schwarz to study the hierarchy of non-urban indigenous dwelling types. Accordingly, six main categories emerge, each with its own distinct social, economic, religious and political structure complemented by its respective settlement pattern and dwelling prototypes:

2

1. Ephemeral or Transient
2. Episodical or Irregular Temporary
3. Periodic or Regular Temporary
4. Seasonal
5. Semi-Permanent
6. Permanent Dwelling Units

The first two categories, namely the ephemeral and episodical dwellings, are inhabited by nomadic, band-type societies based on a hunting-and-gathering existence. The third category, defined as periodic, is characteristic of nomadic tribal societies with a pastoral economy. The fourth group, seasonal, belongs once again to tribal societies but of a semi-nomadic existence based on both pastoral and marginal cultivation pursuits. The fifth type, semi-permanent, is inhabited by members of sedentary folk-societies or hoe-peasants practicing subsistence cultivation. Finally, the sixth type, permanent, belongs to sedentary agricultural societies having a national political social organization and a surplus agricultural economy.

The geographic distribution of these various dwelling forms reveals a general pattern congruous with the particular stage of socio-economic development of their respective societies. Simple societies are predictably found in the least desirable regions while the most complex societies occupy the favourable zones. Thus, ephemeral and episodical dwellings are indigenous to tropical arid deserts, humid equatorial jungles or arctic and sub-arctic barrens. Periodic and seasonal dwellings are predominantly found in arid marginal areas of the sub-tropical and temperate zones. Finally, semi-permanent and permanent dwellings prevail in sub-tropical and temperate regions with adequate precipitation for cultivation.

From the very outset it must be understood that the development of these six categories of dwelling prototypes is rarely a pure sequence model, (1)–(2)–(3)–(4)–(5)–(6). Some intermediate stages are frequently by-passed and this is particularly true of stages (3) and (4), both of which have a pastoral economy at their base; accordingly, a purely agricultural sequence model would be simply (1)–(2)–(5)–(6), namely food gathering and hunting, followed by slash-and-burn primitive cultivation, followed by hoe-peasant cultivation, and ending with surplus agriculture. Of course, there are other conceivable combinations as well, with perhaps only one common denominator, namely that all models start at stage (1).

It must also be borne in mind that there are numerous societies in a transitional stage of development and they consequently occupy a slot between two adjacent categories; moreover, one invariably encounters exceptions, manifesting themselves in either retarded or advanced dwelling forms that do not complement the norm of their respective stages of social development. Recognizing these shortcomings, the above classification is still considered valid to gain a better overview and comprehension of the development of housing.

A study of the hierarchy of dwelling types based on anthropo-geographic and socio-economic criteria reveals many insights into architectural form that were hitherto not clearly perceived. For example, the study indicates that circular floor plans are primordial and consequently must have predated the rectangular shape of certain indigenous shelters. Moreover, it appears that socio-economic development is not complemented by gradual increase in dwelling size or even complexity; indeed, several very large collective dwellings are built by members of simple social organizations. These are but a few unexpected observations that emerged along with many others which were logically predictable.

This study deals with contemporary shelters rather than with historic or prehistoric dwelling forms. The objective—to illustrate the development stages of housing by means of existing dwellings inhabited by living people—is still possible today, but probably not for very long. Simple social organizations disappear through acculturation at an ever increasing rate and with this phenomenon will vanish the opportunity to present a "history" of housing using examples of contemporary indigenous dwellings.

1

EPHEMERAL
OR TRANSIENT DWELLINGS

The most simple dwelling types are ephemeral or transient dwellings. As their name indicates, the effective use period of these dwellings forms is usually not more than a few days since their inhabitants are food gatherers and lowly hunters constantly on the move in an endless pursuit of better hunting grounds.

The social structure of these primitive people is characterized by small groups called "bands," which groups consist of members of associated families living together and maintaining face-to-face relations under nomadic conditions. The bands are self-regulating in a completely informal manner and leadership is assumed as occasion demands by a skilled hunter or by an older man; these headmen have no special powers and are considered only first among equals. The band is of necessity a cooperative, identifiable, self-contained social entity.

The economic success of primitive hunters and food gatherers depends upon the cooperative activity of every individual and family within the group; the economic unit is thus the band, and the success of the elemental human way of life is group success. Men on the elemental level feel a sense of ownership of the wild plants and animals on their territory, but their degree of control over these plants and animals is small; hence, the notion of property owned by groups and by individuals is either non-existent or limited to a few material possessions such as clothing and hunting gear. As a result, men on the elemental level of hunting and food-gathering economy get along very well with one another, in families, and in groups.

Since primitive nomads do not produce food but subsist on the game and plants that nature provides, they must of necessity leave their campsite as soon as the food resources within walking distance of their dwellings are exhausted. It must be noted that primitive nomads do not roam aimlessly, but migrate within recognized band territories; indeed, their movements often follow a seasonal pattern complementing variations in food-gathering opportunities. Essentially their mode of life is a precarious one depending greatly on an intimate knowledge of their respective territory; they must know the location of water-holes, they must know where certain edible plants grow and where game can best be stalked. In some instances, a few hunters and food gatherers increase their supply of food by burning the bush at certain seasons to inhibit the growth of undesired vegetation, by protecting seedlings, or by channeling watercourses to provide better irrigation to a particular area to encourage an abundance of wild edible plants.

Food gathering and hunting as the sole means of subsistence represents also the most primitive phase in the hierarchical system of social evolution preceding the pastoral and agricultural stages of human societies. In primordial times all human beings lived entirely on wild plants and game. Of necessity, in a purely food-gathering and hunting society, population densities had to be sparse. People lived essentially in ecological balance with the natural environment, affecting it in ways and to degrees no different than did large animals; their numbers were rigidly controlled by food supply determined by forces over which they had little, if any, control. Depending on prevailing climatic conditions, it is now estimated that an area of 4,500 to 320,000 acres was required per person for subsistence in this mode of life.

The precise form of prehistoric ephemeral dwellings is not and may never be known, but it is not likely that these dwellings were very different from the transient dwellings used at present by the few lowly hunters and food-gathering bands still roaming in some isolated parts of our globe, since their life-style represents an Old Stone Age culture that has survived into our time.

The dwelling forms of primitive nomads have several basic characteristics in addition to their ephemeral nature. They are simple shelters, small in size, constructed solely of building materials collected in the immediate vicinity of the campsite. These shelters are erected in a very short period of time, usually a few hours, and the workmanship is so unskilled that only the most elementary form of interior climate control is provided. The shelters are circular in shape and are enclosed by a beehive type of roof structure; they have no vertical walls, no windows and no smoke holes but only an open entranceway without a door. The low interior space of the ephemeral dwelling is not subdivided into use areas.

One exception to the prototypical ephemeral dwelling are the homes of the Tassaday. These recently discovered bands inhabit the impenetrable rain forest of the southern Philippines and live in three limestone and conglomerate caves about five hundred feet up a mountain slope. Their sedentary way of life is a departure from the nomad norm and is made possible by the abundance of food supply in their jungle territory over which the Tassaday regularly range, a territory which is remarkably small and extends not further than five miles from their caves.

Bushmen Werf

Bushmen Skerm

AFRICAN BUSHMEN SKERM

The grass SKERMS of the African Bushmen living in the arid wastes of the Kalahari Desert may serve as a prototype for ephemeral dwellings. Bushmen of the Kung group follow an aboriginal pattern of independent nomadic life relying on collective hunting-gathering. Since food is scarce during most of the year in their territory, Bushmen are constantly migrating in search of new food supply. Usually a band consists of about 25 to 30 persons. The bow and poisoned arrows, and club, are their main hunting weapons. A digging stick is used by women to dig up roots. Men hunt, make weapons and prepare skins for loincloths; women gather food, build the huts, gather wood and kindle

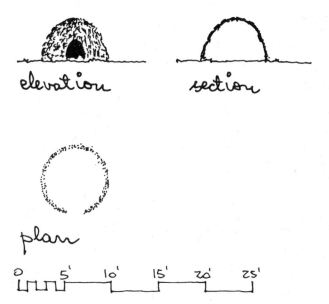

elevation   section

plan

0   5'   10'   15'   20'   25'

Bushmen Skerm

11

Bushmen Skerm

the fire, cook and keep the campsite clean. The small grass shelters of the Bushmen are erected by the women in one or two hours and are abandoned after a few days when the band moves on. The building procedure commences with the gathering of grass until a large pile is collected. The women then break a few branches from a nearby tree and thrust them upright into the ground; the branches are then arched together to form a rudimentary skeleton of a structure which can support the grass covering; each shelter is then tied once round with a sinew string.

Elders, and single men or women of the band are sometimes left without a hut; to give themselves a place of their own, they thrust a little branch upright into the ground and place their few belongings beside it. Bushmen prefer to sleep in the open beside the fire and frequently store only their few personal possessions in the skerms.

The various grass shelters of the band are usually accommodated under the branches of a single large tree; this encampment is called a WERF. Campsites are always built within easy reach of food although a mile or so away from a waterhole in order not to interfere with local game. The huts are usually clustered together without a fixed pattern and entrances may point in any direction. However, the placement of the KAO, the hut of the unmarried young men, is always placed to the east of the headman's dwelling.

BaMbuti Pygmy Hut

BAMBUTI PYGMY HUT

Another example of an ephemeral dwelling type is the BaMbuti Pygmy beehive hut. The BaMbuti are forest people inhabiting Africa's Ituri Forest, a vast expanse of dense, dark, damp and inhospitable jungle. Their name for the forest is *Ndura*, a word that also means the entire world.

The BaMbuti hunt the game of this region and gather the wild fruits, roots and mushrooms that grow in abundance there. They are small people, averaging less than four-and-a-half feet in height; they are powerful and tough and have the ability to run swiftly and silently, characteristics that are essential for survival in a hunting-and-gathering existence. The BaMbuti roam the forest in hunting bands consisting of at least six to seven individual families, each with its own hunting net; only in this way can they have an efficient nethunt, with the women and children driving the animals into the long circle of nets, joined end to end. In addition to nets, spears as well as bows and poisoned arrows are used in hunting game and birds. BaMbuti clothing is minimal and consists of a simple loincloth made of bark.

Once again the construction of the shelter is the responsibility of the women. Crouching in a squatting position they drive young saplings (fito) into the ground with sharp thrusts, each time in exactly the same place until they are firm in the ground. When a circle of straight saplings surrounds them, the women stand up and skillfully bend the fito over their heads, twisting and twining smaller saplings across until a lattice framework is formed.

After the framework is completed, the women gather large heart-shaped mongongo leaves collected by the men and slit the stalks toward the end, like clothespins, hooking two or three of them together and hanging them on the framework like tiles, overlapping each other to form a waterproof covering. Sometimes there are as many as four women working on the thatching of

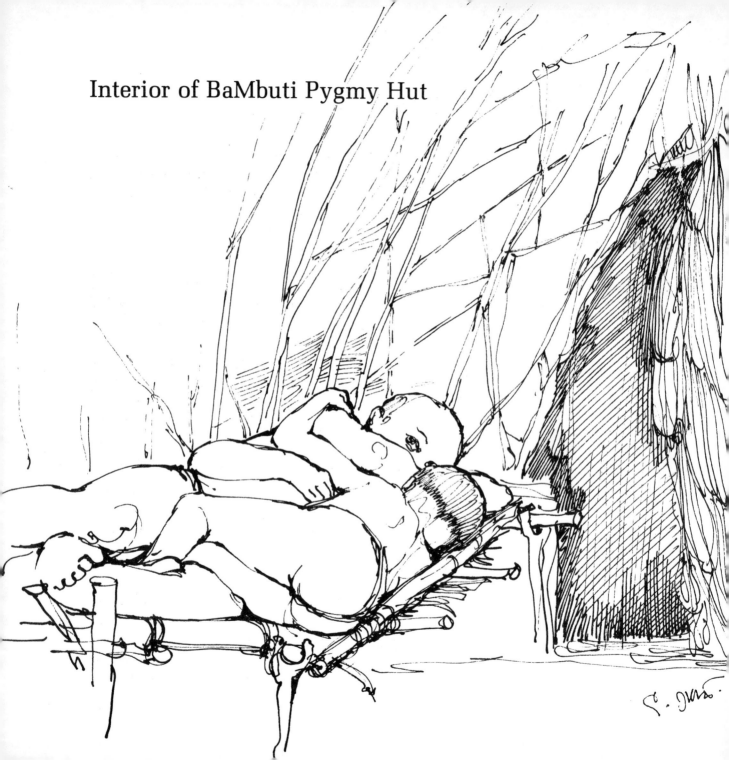

Interior of BaMbuti Pygmy Hut

a hut, some hanging leaves from the outside, working upward, others working from the inside, pushing the leaves through the lattice and fastening leaves from the top down. The entrance is simply a gap in the framework of the shelter.

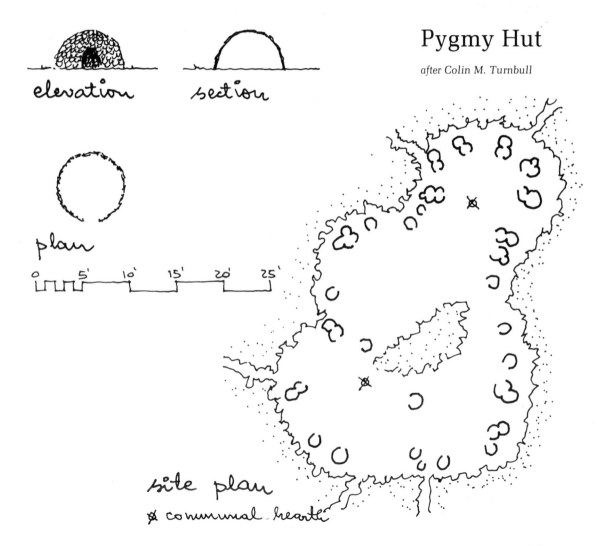

Pygmy Hut

after Colin M. Turnbull

elevation   section

plan

0   5'   10'   15'   20'   25'

site plan
⊠ communal hearth

At first the huts leak when it rains, but once the leaves have settled down, not even the hardest rain can penetrate the roof. It remains watertight until the leaves get old and dried out and begin to curl.

The BaMbuti are clean people and do not like to sit down on the bare ground. Most often they sit on logs, even on the end of a log that is sticking out of a fire; they will sometimes pull a mongongo leaf from the roof of the nearest hut and sit daintily on that. They also make simple chairs by cutting four sticks, each about three-and-a-half feet long, and twisting a vine thong around the middle of the bundle; when the bundle is stood on the ground with a turn of the hand, the ends are splayed out and a seat is formed.

The bedstead of the BaMbuti may consist of a layer of dry leaves or sticks placed directly on the ground. Also used, however, is an elevated bed made of sticks lashed together and bound by vine thongs to a frame.

A fire is normally made outside the entrance of the beehive hut. During a spell of rain, the fire is moved temporarily inside the hut, but as soon as the rain stops it is rekindled in its original position outside.

Usually the campsite (APA) of the BaMbuti is erected in a forest clearing near a stream. The huts are placed near the edge of the clearing and depending on the number of huts required to house the hunting band, one or two circular communal open spaces are defined by their position. The entrances of the huts point in different directions, usually towards friends or relatives, but never towards the forest; if a woman has a grudge against a neighbour or a dislike for someone who has built a hut opposite hers, she will rearrange the entrance to her own hut to face another direction, or move her hut altogether. Since little jealousies are inevitable in small communities and since most of the women are continually adding to their huts, the layout of the apa is in a continuous state of change during the BaMbuti's stay of about one month in the same camp.

ARUNTA HUT

The third example of an ephemeral dwelling type is the hut of the Arunta, Australia's aboriginal people.

The Arunta live in the desert environment of central Australia and subsist through a food-gathering and hunting economy. Small bands consisting of one to three families forage the desert in a constant quest for food. The men's sole hunting weapons are spears and bommerangs; a digging stick with a crude point is used by the women to dig for roots and tubers. Despite the often bitter night cold, the Arunta have no clothing or even wraps to cover themselves while asleep; on cold nights, the family huddles with its dogs for warmth. Indeed, they note the temperature by the number of dogs per man required to feel comfortable; thus, a four-dog night is unusually cold.

The Arunta live in crude shelters made by lacing branches into a low dome-shaped framework and thatching this lattice structure with grass, leaves, reeds or whatever is available. They use no furniture. A small fire is usually kept burning in front of or inside the shelter; people huddle close around it.

A deceased Arunta's hut is burned and his few personal belongings are destroyed; the members of the band move to a new campsite, fearful of the spirit which is believed to stay near the grave until a purification ceremony is performed later.

The typical encampment of the Arunta is a few huts in close proximity. If the camp is very temporary, the families of the band shelter themselves from the wind with a rough lean-to or windscreen of shrubs.

There are still other examples of ephemeral dwellings. In Asia, for example, the nomadic bands of the Semang living on the Malay Peninsula inhabit a simple dome-shaped hut consisting of a framework of light branches covered

Arunta Hut

with interlaced rattan leaves. Their clothing is merely a loincloth, and raised bedsteads of bamboo are commonly the only furniture used.

Food-gathering and hunting societies no longer exist on the American Continent. But not many decades ago, Yaguans roamed in southern Argentina and Utes in Utah; the former lived in conical brush huts, while the latter inhabited flimsy brush "wickiups".

Arunta Hut, Australia

Yaguan Hut, South America

2

EPISODICAL OR IRREGULAR
TEMPORARY DWELLINGS

The second and more advanced prototypes of simple dwellings are also inhabited by food gatherers and hunters living a band-type of social organization. But, in contrast to the former group, these nomadic bands are skilled hunters or fishermen living in a richer environment than that of the lowly hunters; they are primarily hunters (or fishermen) and only secondarily food gatherers. Although their shelter is still erected within an hour or two, the use period of an episodical dwelling extends generally to several weeks.

Advanced hunters and gatherers also live primarily in ecological balance with the natural environment. Although they do not have direct control of this natural environment, they do have a greater effect on it than primitive hunters; they are the dominant animals in the ecological communities of which they are a part.

The social structure of these primitive societies does not differ greatly from that of the lowly hunters and food gatherers. Both societies are characterized by small groups in which all interpersonal relations are face-to-face interactions. This interaction of the members of closed groups is by necessity based on involuntary associations and their interrelationship is often many-stranded; in other words, members of primitive bands seldom have the choice of associating with preferred persons and their relationship to each other can take many forms. A father-son relationship, for example, can also be teacher-pupil, chieftain-subordinate, healer–patient, high-priest–worshiper relationship, etc.

Differences in cultural inheritance and mode of life rather than in social structure set the skilled hunters apart from the primitive hunters. They have more personal belongings in the form of clothing, tools and weapons. They have vehicles such as sleds to transport goods and frequently have domesticated working animals such as dogs to pull sleds or travois.

These differences may appear to be slight, but nevertheless they are enough to bring about considerable changes in dwelling forms. The foremost characteristic of a more advanced society of hunters or fishermen is its adjustment to adverse climatic conditions; the function of climate control in dwellings is more sophisticated and is complemented by the degree of skill manifested in the design of clothing. Indeed, it is not seldom that these band societies have two distinguishable dwelling types, one inhabited during the winter months and the other during the summer. A second characteristic of these temporary dwellings is their relative size; both the surface area of the dwelling as well as the height of the interior are considerably greater than in the ephemeral shelter. The interior is divided into sleeping zones and a cooking area with a designated place for the fire or hearth. Sleeping inside the shelter and making a fire indoors are both definite traits of skilled hunters. At least some building materials of an irregular temporary dwelling are reused and transported from one encampment to another. Finally, an obvious characteristic setting the episodical dwelling apart from the ephemeral one is the greater variety that exists in their form.

Inuit Igloo

INUIT IGLOO

Perhaps the most fascinating prototypes of an episodical dwelling is the IGLOO built by the Inuit (Eskimo) living in the treeless tundra of the Canadian North.

The Inuit have two—and sometimes even more—distinct settlements determined primarily by the basic economic activity of the season. The longest period of residence is at the winter site which is normally located on a sheltered bay or on the lee side of some eminence. Here, the Inuit builds his igloo, a dome-shaped snow house serving as the winter home. At the very outset, the igloo builder has to locate snow, wind-packed to the right consistency, neither too hard and icy, nor too soft and powdery. Not just any snow will do. Then, with a long knife of bone, ivory or metal he cuts rectangular snow blocks measuring about three feet long, twenty inches wide and from six to ten inches thick and slightly bevelled so as to corbel when laid in a continuous spiral, thus forming a dome. The first step in the building process is to lay a number of blocks on edge until the circular base of the wall is complete; thereafter, the Inuit trims the top of the base to enable the spiral-laying of consecutive snow blocks.

Working from the inside, the builder now lays one snow block next to another in upward spiraling rows, each block tipped inward slightly to narrow the circle. Thus a dome structure results, ingenious in its method of construction, since scaffoldings to support the dome during construction are made superfluous by the spiraling rows which prevent the walls from caving in.

When the dome is almost complete and only the key block is missing, the builder cuts himself an exit passage near the bottom of the hut. From the outside he lowers the last block, the so-called key block, into place. (The Inuit can cut blocks very rapidly and with his eye can measure their size to such accuracy that the blocks almost invariably fit their intended places.)

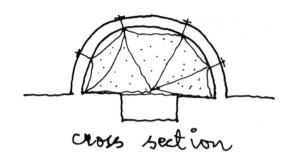

cross section

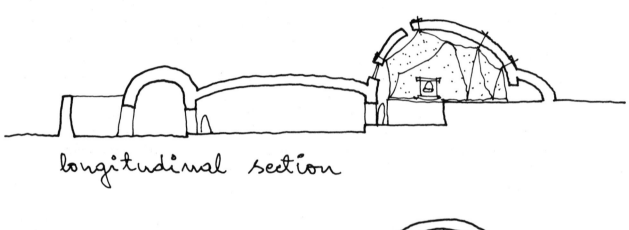

longitudinal section

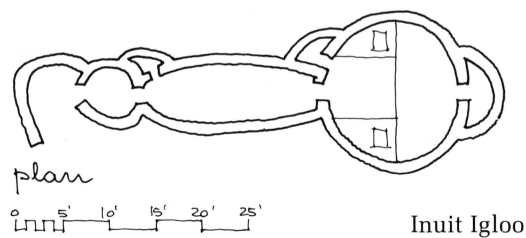

plan

0   5'   10'   15'   20'   25'

Inuit Igloo

To complete the igloo, the builder constructs a low vaulted tunnel or passageway in front of the entrance which has to be negotiated on hands and knees. The entrance tunnel is low and often quite long, with its floor set one or two feet lower than the main igloo; these measures are now and then augmented by a sharp bend in the passageway in order to further minimize or even exclude any draughts of cold air.

A window located above the entrance and consisting of a sheet of ice or made of the translucent membrane of a seal's intestine lights the igloo. Above the window and near the top of the dome there is a small hole for ventilation.

Once all the building is finished, blubber lamps are lit in the interior. The igloo is evacuated and all openings are sealed including the entranceway. In this way the lamps heat up the interior space and the inside wall surfaces begin to melt. Due to the inherent characteristics of the dome shape, excess water from the sweating walls does not drop to the floor but slowly tickles downward on the inside surface until it is totally absorbed by less saturated wall sections in the lower parts of the walls.

Inuit Igloo

In a short while the entire inside surface is permeated with moisture. As soon as this stage of moisture saturation is reached, the main doorway and the ventilation hole near the top of the dome are opened and cold air rushes into the dwelling while the warm air escapes through the vent. The inside surface is suddenly chilled and the water-permeated walls freeze solid into a monolithic structure. Similarly, prolonged occupancy invariably makes an igloo more substantial since the occasional slight melting inside inevitably freezes again. Igloos are known to have obtained such rigidity in this fashion that they easily supported the massive body of a wandering polar bear.

Igloos may be built as large as fifteen feet in diameter and more than ten feet high at the centre. A sleeping platform raised well above the floor occupies the rear half of the floor plan. This large platform is made of snow and is covered with moss or willow twigs overlaid with caribou furs. On both sides of the igloo's entrance we find smaller platforms. On top of these side benches the Inuit places his cooking utensils as well as the shallow saucer-shaped stone lamps. By burning animal fat, such as seal blubber, in these lamps, the igloo dweller solves the problem of heat and light throughout the long winter season.

Drifting snow will invariably pile over and around the igloo, protecting it further from the below freezing temperatures of the outdoors. Moreover, insulation of the interior is often enhanced by lining walls and ceilings with hides and sealskins; these are held in place by cords passing through the snow blocks and secured by toggles. Not only do the hides themselves improve the comfort of the igloo, but the air space created between the exterior walls and the hides materially augments the insulation of the snow house. The main door leading to the igloo is also usually made of suspended hides and frequently a double-door effect is obtained through the multiple use of several hides. Even when extreme low temperatures prevail out of doors, the inside of the igloo presents a comfortable environment and the Inuit may remain in their snow huts for several days in a row.

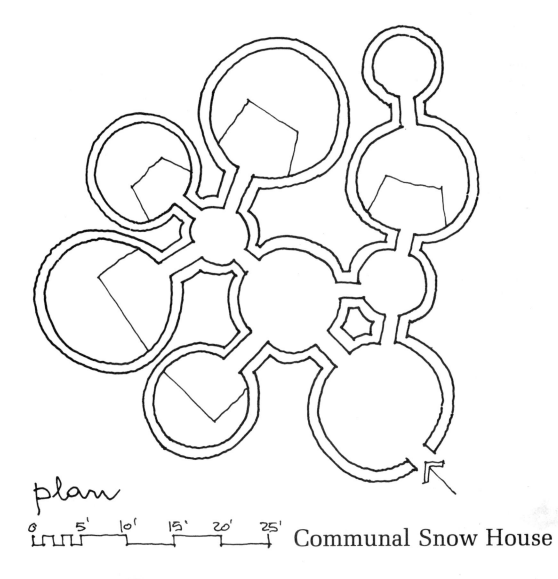

plan

0 5' 10' 15' 20' 25'

Communal Snow House

Given the proper snow, a man can erect within an hour's time an igloo large enough to shelter his entire family. As a rule, the snow houses are built for one family only, but in certain territories, communal snow houses may be found. These compound structures consist of a number of round huts linked to each other with short vaulted tunnels. Most of the dome structures are dwelling units similar to the main chamber of the igloo described above. Other dome-shaped structures are store rooms and/or assembly rooms where all the inhabitants of the communal house can gather.

The igloo is abandoned when the sun begins to melt the dwelling. In any case, however, the Inuit is now ready to leave his winter settlement to move to his spring hunting grounds and will live in seal tents congruous to this period of nomadic life. The abandoned igloo, on the other hand, melts away, leaving no trace for posterity to reflect upon.

Inuit Seal Tent

TUNGUS TENT

Another type of episodical dwelling is used by the Northern Tungus inhabiting the great expanse of eastern Siberia.

The nomadic Tungus are both reindeer herders and hunters. In winter they roam the so-called taiga or northern forested areas covered with mosses, lichens, shrubs and dwarf willows, all of which are food for reindeer. Snowfall is relatively light, but temperatures can reach as low as –80°F. The herds must be constantly on the move because the snow becomes packed from the trampling of the herd and the animals cannot dig through it. In summer the herd is moved to the tundra for pasture where it must fatten on grass, willow shoots, lichens and reeds to withstand the harsh eight to nine months of the long winter season.

The reindeer are milked, but in the best condition they give not more than one pint of milk a day after suckling their fawn. Reindeer are also used as mounts and pack animals. The herd is not shepherded; it is left to itself to find pasture and water.

The basic economic unit of the Tungus is the family, augmented perhaps by an older surviving relative of the husband; it is a small tent household. By necessity, their dwelling is an easily transportable home and resembles in form and structure a teepee. The conical framework consists of a number of poles leaning against each other. The winter tent is covered with skins and the summer with birch bark. With the exception of the smoke holes, the tent is kept tightly closed and a fire is continually kept alive in order to keep out the intense cold in winter and to inhibit insects in summer. Consequently, the interior is always smoky.

The section to the right of the entrance is reserved for the husband and his wife; the left side is occupied by the oldest son; the area opposite the entrance is reserved for the spirits or for an eminent male visitor.

There is a division of labour between males and females. The principal day-to-day activity of the male is hunting and trapping, in addition to other outdoor tasks such as loading of pack animals, slaughtering and skinning as well as cutting firewood. The women take care of children, cook, milk reindeer, dress the skins and make clothing and tent covers.

The Tungus move about within a defined clan territory with a sparse population density of about one person for every one hundred square miles.

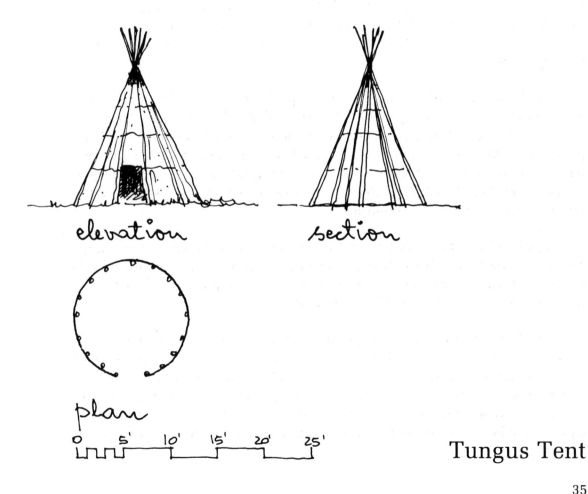

elevation   section

plan

0   5'   10'   15'   20'   25'

Tungus Tent

COMMUNAL EPISODICAL DWELLINGS

Other contemporary types of episodical dwellings are those inhabited by simple segmentary or sub-tribes with a decentralized system of autonomous communities. Coupled with hunting and food collecting, these sub-tribes practice "slash-and-burn" cultivation, a form of cultivation predominantly associated with a tropical rain forest mode of life; it represents the simplest, most ancient and least productive use of cropland. Only a few implements such as the axe, the machete and a digging-planting stick are employed; moreover, in the absence of domesticated draft animals, labour energy is provided solely by human effort.

Slash-and-burn cultivation entails several steps. First, a patch of forest is cleared by burning off the existing vegetation cover. Second, crops are planted in the clearing without additional manuring other than the mineral nutrients provided by the ashes of the burned vegetation. Third, the plot is cultivated for one or two years until the soil ceases to be productive. Fourth, the plot is abandoned and a new plot cleared for cultivation, usually in a distant location offering better hunting opportunities.

The "fields" of the slash-and-burn cultivators invariably remain full of stumps and logs during their cultivation and crops are often grown mixed; fields seldom exceed one acre in area. This short-term use of forest plots is called MILPA in Latin American and LADANG in Indonesia.

Two requirements are inherent to slash-and-burn cultivation, namely, a large collective labour force in the absence of plow and draft animals, a large amount of reserve land to allow for the customary fallows of eight years or longer, and adequate hunting territory. Consequently, population densities are frequently less than 10 persons per square mile—or 1 person per 64 acres—if the equilibrium between man and nature in this type of subsistence is to be maintained.

Although the interpersonal relationships of slash-and-burn cultivators are similar to those of skilled hunters, other characteristics such as the greater stability of their settlements bring about some changes in the form of their dwellings as well as in the number and kind of their personal possessions. In keeping with their collective economy, their dwellings are single detached large communal structures, frequently of an oval plan and resembling a large haystack situated in the middle of an oval forest clearing.

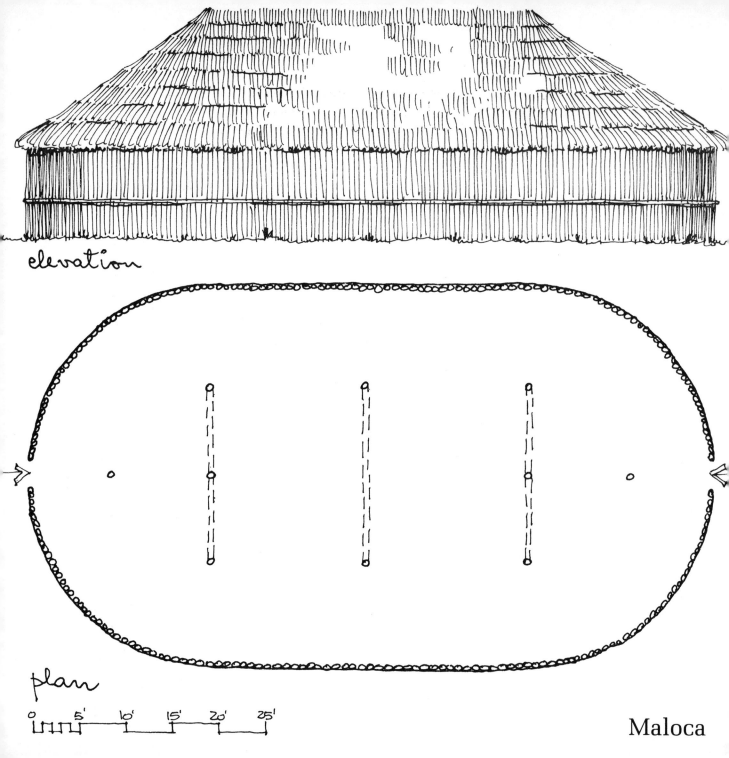

elevation

plan

0   5'   10'   15'   20'   25'

Maloca

ERIGBAAGTSA MALOCA

The MALOCAS of the various native tribes, such as the Erigbaagtsa Indians living in the northwestern part of the Amazon basin, illustrate well the characteristics of communal shelters inhabited by slash-and-burn cultivators.

In building a maloca, a large open space is carefully leveled in the centre of the forest clearing. The main supporting structure is then erected—three pairs of large trunks with connecting beams, one pair located at each end and a third one in the middle of the long sides. Between these, smaller posts braced with horizontal members, secured entirely by liana thongs, are introduced to complement the structure. The roof and sides are thatched with thick layers of babussu palm fronds.

Depending on the number of families inhabiting it, the dimensions of the maloca vary, but it is not unusual for the length to exceed one hundred feet, its width sixty feet and its height thirty feet. Essentially, the maloca is a large dark one-room shelter with the central part reserved for public receptions and dances. Small fires flicker on the ground and the hammocks of each family are slung from the rafters adjacent to each individual fire. There are no separating partitions or windows; several entrances tightly closed with thick palm frond door panels shelter the inhabitants from gnat-size blood-sucking flies called Piums. To escape these pests, the near-naked dwellers of the maloca spend much of their lives indoors and venture into daylight only to hunt and fish, bathe, and fetch wood and water. They work their fields of corn, manioc and cotton before dawn.

Life within the maloca is communalistic; all participate in building the house and tilling the plot; only weapons are personal property. Harmony invariably prevails in their community where all men are blood relations. Everybody is friendly and soft-spoken. Women spin cotton into cord for hammocks, cook monkey meat or wild pork, roast corn and lie in hammocks tending their

Waura Maloca

babies. Men and boys squat on tree trunks which are placed to form a rectangle and chat while making bows and arrows and feather decorations. This log rectangle is reserved for menfolk; here they eat their meals together and tend a fire in the centre of the rectangle.

The nights are cool, but everybody sleeps naked; small children sleep with their mothers, older ones in their own hammocks and young boys sleep apart with the unmarried men.

Another example of communal shelters is the BOHIO of the Motilone Indians who live in the Catatumbo River area of Venezuela. The bohios resemble giant haystacks also, paths radiating like spider's legs from its twelve doors. The interiors of these communal houses are smoky and crowded since their inhabitants often number seventy or more.

The Piaroa Indians of the Orinoco River jungle also inhabit bohio-type palm-thatched, peak-roofed communal houses.

WAI-WAI COMMUNAL DWELLING

Like other tropical forest Indians, the Wai-Wai of British Guiana also inhabit communal dwellings.

The Wai-Wai live in small isolated groups and practice a simple, rugged pattern of communal agriculture augmented by hunting and fishing. Land is cleared in the jungle by felling trees and burning repeatedly the dense tree-strewn field. The communal crops include cassava, sugar cane, bananas, pineapples and tubers, all planted indiscriminately among the unburned stumps and tree trunks cluttering the field. The fields are seldom used for more than two or three years because the soil wears out. Consequently, the Wai-Wai have to abandon their settlement and move on to a new clearing; they seldom return to a previous site.

The indigenous communal dwelling of the Wai-Wai is a single circular and cone-shaped hut with walls built of vertical poles supporting a large thatched roof structure. The hut is not divided by partitions, but each family has a designated area between two roof posts. Each compartment has its own hearth for cooking and the warmth required at night. Sleeping hammocks are draped between the hut's posts with the woman's hammock slung beneath her husband's. Dogs, their only domesticated animals, are tethered on special platforms along the walls and are walked as pets on a leash. Cassava cakes and smoked meat are piled on racks; feather ornaments, gourds of palm oil, baskets and arrows are hung from the ceiling. Since there is no chimney, smoke escapes through apertures in the thatched roof.

Labour is usually divided between the sexes. Men build the communal house, they hunt, fish, clear land, plant and sometimes help women harvest the crops; they also weave hammocks, baskets and cloth. Women tend children, cook, fetch water, chop firewood and keep the fire going all night, weave bead aprons, spin cotton and make cassava graters.

elevation

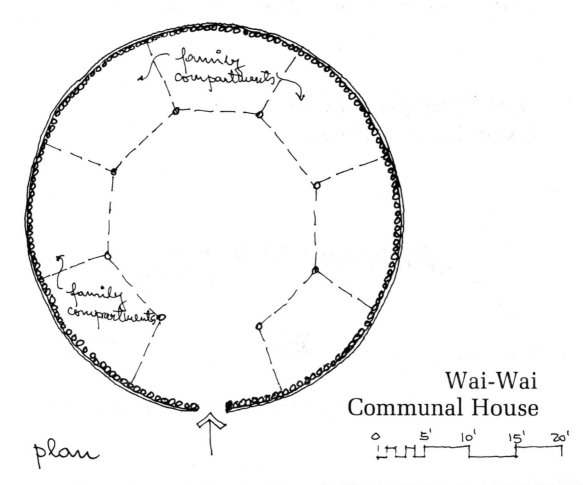

family
compartments

family
compartments

plan

Wai-Wai
Communal House

0   5'   10'   15'   20'

Their clothing consists only of a loincloth, but they are very fastidious about their appearance. Their bodies are invariably decorated with plant juice to ward off harmful spirits; they wear earrings, necklaces of red beads, armbands of white and legbands of blue and white beads. Their hair is combed and dressed with palm-nut oil, then fashioned into a tight pigtail adorned with feathers.

The Wai-Wai seldom penetrate the jungle and then only to hunt. They fish by poisoning the water or shoot larger fish with arrows. Their highway is the river and their transportation mode a dugout canoe. Distances are measured in paddling time or by the number of bends in the river.

Other Examples of Communal Episodical Dwellings

Camayura Communal House, Rio Xingu, Brasil

Caraya Communal House, Brasil

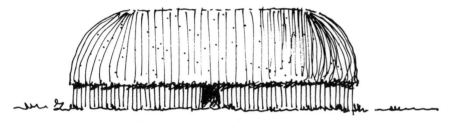

Paressi Communal House, Brasil

Yecuana Communal House, French Guiana

3

PERIODIC OR REGULAR TEMPORARY DWELLINGS

Shelters reflecting the third evolutionary stage of dwelling forms are inhabited by pastoral nomads comprising the tribal social organization with a number of bands or other sub-groups. Tribal societies represent a category of cultural development, intermediate in complexity, between the primitive hunters/food gatherers and agrarian societies; pastoral nomadism is essentially the ecological converse of forest slash-and-burn cultivation since the former represents an adaptation to open semi-arid grassland and the latter to humid tropical rain forest.

A tribe is a body of people of common derivation and custom in possession and control of its own extensive territory; it is characterized by widespread cohesion and some centralization at higher levels. Thus, tribal people frequently develop chiefdoms. This hierarchy is needed to blunt the frequent collisions between neighbouring camps, to minimize competition over pasture, and finally, to coordinate annual cycles in proper relation to pastoral resources.

The main characteristics of tribal societies which set them apart from hunters and food gatherers are primarily their pastoral economy, their homogeneous culture and the possession of some form of political organization. In the more advanced stages of pastoral nomadism, there appears to be an increasing dependence on settled agriculture. However, this dependence is facultative only; in other words, it may, but need not, occur, a relationship which is in great contrast to their obligate relations to their livestock upon which survival depends.

Although some tribes depend to a certain extent on hunting and food gathering, most pastoral nomads depend solely on domesticated livestock for subsistence. Their cyclical or seasonal migration pattern depends on the topography and climate prevalent in their established territory. Some groups, with their live-stock, migrate hundreds of miles between their winter quarters in the south and their summer pastures in the north; others move only a few miles from their winter settlements at the foot of a mountain range and the summer grazing areas on the higher slopes of the mountain. Population densities range mainly between one and five persons per square mile or the equivalent of one person per 125 to 640 acres.

The ideal household in many pastoral tribes includes two or more married couples and their children, the extended family. If the polygynous family is the rule, a man's sons ordinarily break away upon marriage and establish a neolocal residence.

Climatic forces and the nomadic life of these tribal societies are the predominant formative forces determining the shape, structure and construction method of their dwellings. In some instances, because of the intense cold in winter, the shape of the dwelling must have a minimum of exposed surface, and in order to withstand high winds, the structure must have maximum stability. A dome-shaped shelter consisting of a skeleton membrane lends additional strength to the shelter. These building materials also possess a low heat storage capacity which is advantageous in winter when a quick heat response to the fire is required, and also in summer, when shade and ventilation are easily afforded during the long warm days. The portable dwellings of the pastoral nomads must consist of lightweight materials which can be transported from one periodic settlement to the other with the help of pack animals.

MONGOLIAN YURT

An excellent example of a portable dwelling used by nomadic tribes living in the rich steppe lands of Asia is the Mongolian YURT.

The yurt is an ingenious and weatherproof dwelling which affords to its occupants a remarkable degree of protection against the inclemency of weather and in particular agaainst the strong winds of the continental steppe. The yurt has a circular plan with a diameter of 12 to 20 feet. Its vertical walls are about four feet high and consist of a lightweight willow latticework that can be folded up like a children's safety gate for ease of transportation. This latticework in its expanded form is lashed to poles firmly fixed in the ground. To the top of the yurt's walls are fastened curved poles radiating from the centre and fitted into a wooden ring of four-foot diameter; this compression ring at the top of the yurt also serves as the smoke hole. Because of the yurt's shape, wind pressure acting upon the structure results in anchoring it more firmly to the ground. At times, to increase the solidity of this light-weight structure, a heavy stone is suspended on a rope from the central wooden ring.

Over the entire framework of the yurt, large pieces of heavy felt called *mundahs* are fastened, sometimes in two or even three layers, with air space in between in order to increase the comfort of the interior. A felt curtain, often richly embroidered, is hung over the door that inevitably faces south. The door curtain as well as the wall panels can be rolled up to give better ventilation if so desired. Curtains are also hung in the interior and can be let down to form separate compartments. Both the setting up and taking down of the yurt are always done by the women.

A fire of argol (dried yak or camel dung cakes) is made in the centre of the yurt and is surrounded by dry stunted brush. The smoke of the fire escapes through the central hole in the roof; when necessary, the smoke hole can be closed by a piece of felt drawn across by a string. Even in severe weather, the interior of the Mongolian yurt offers its occupants adequate warmth.

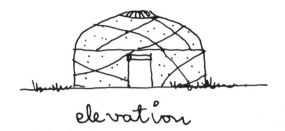

elevation

section

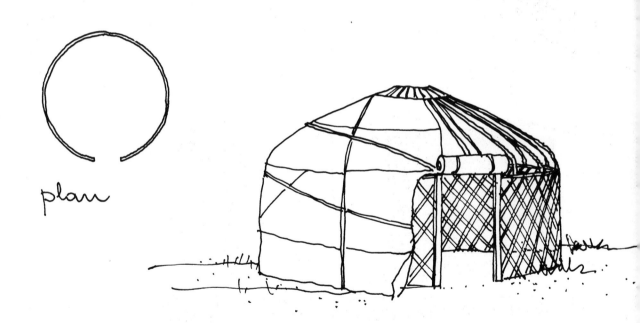

plan

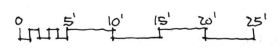

0   5'   10'   15'   20'   25'

Mongolian Yurt

after James Marston Fitch

Mongolian Yurt

Although the structure is lightweight, the covering material stretched across the yurt is cumbersome and heavy. This could mean a great disadvantage for a nomadic people; however, pack animals such as camels, horses and cattle provide sufficient means of transportation to carry not only the portable dwelling but also the rugs and other household and personal belongings of the tribe.

TUAREG HUT

A second example of a periodic shelter is the Tuareg hutlike tent used by pastoral nomads living in the Sahara Desert.

The Tuaregs who live on the fringes of the desert, are related to Berbers. Tuareg men are veiled, but not their women; they are usually very poor, subsisting on a meagre diet of goat's milk, as a staple with wheat and millet added. Owen Lattimore's definition of "a pure nomad being a poor nomad" aptly describes the condition of the Tuaregs.

The Tuareg tent consists of a dozen slim poles and laths made from acacia or palm-leaf stems bent and laced to form a framework not unlike the skeleton of a dome-shaped hut. Grass mats and skins are thrown over this framework and tied down securely. The sole furnishing of these tents consists of a couch of branches built fifteen inches off the ground and occupying nearly the whole floor. On this couch, the family sits and sleeps.

Tuaregs own few personal possessions and few cooking utensils, but one must remember than an accumulation of worldly goods beyond a certain number restricts the pastorist's freedom of movement and threatens his mobility.

Tuareg Hut

BEDOUIN TENT

A third example of a periodic and portable dwelling is the Bedouin tent. In fact, the word *Bedouin* means "man of the tent".

Bedouins are hardy desert herdsmen living in both Western Asia and North Africa. They raise camels and migrate with their livestock in the severe environments of the endless deserts of Arabia and the Sahara. In poor grazing seasons, namely during the height of summer, Bedouins are forced to camp near towns or form settlements which provide access to the stubble of harvested fields; they also depend to a large degree on towns for vital manufactures ranging from metal utensils and weapons through clothing and footwear.

The typical Bedouin tent has a supporting structure of vertical poles, sometimes forked, and ridgepoles. A corase cover og goat's-hair strips sewn together and dyed black is stretched over the poles. This awning-like cover may be pegged down at the back or banked with stones and sand if cross ventilation is not desired.

A woolen carpet hung from the ridge divides the tent into two parts; the area to the right of the entrance is occupied by women and children, that to the left is the domaine of men and guests. Within the tent, a rough mat or carpet is spread on the ground. The contents of the tent are scant and consist mainly of cooking utensils, pack saddles, water skins, wheat bags, halters, bowls and various weapons.

The average length of the Bedouin tent is twenty to thirty feet, the depth not more than ten, and the height five to seven feet. A sheik's tent, however, may attain a length of forty feet.

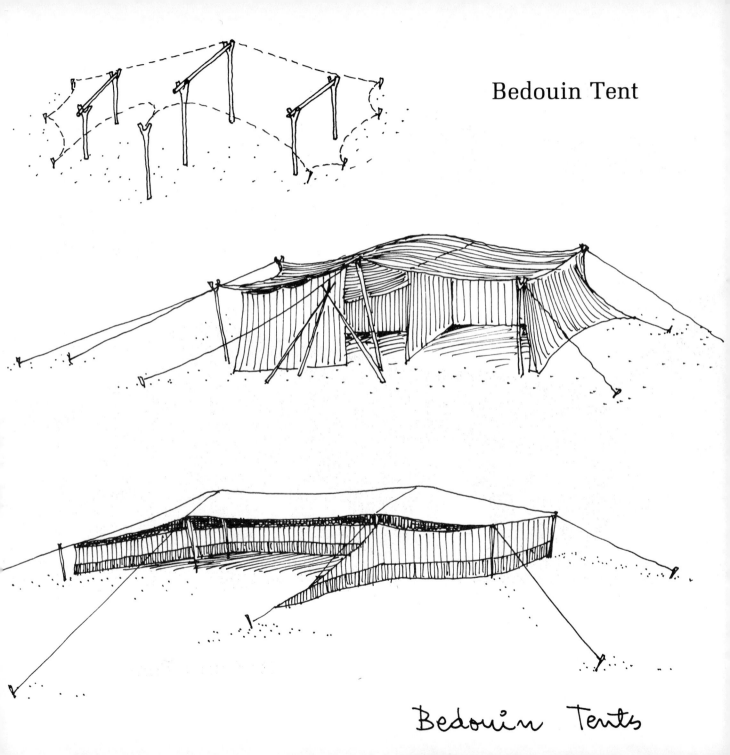

Bedouin Tent

Bedouin Tents

Bedouin Tent

4

SEASONAL DWELLINGS

The fourth group of dwellings are those inhabited by semi-nomads practicing some form of cultivation, namely planting crops and harvesting them, between seasonal migrations in their quest for survival as hunters and stock breeders. The social organization that forms the basis of semi-nomadism is a tribal community usually consisting of a number of clans with a strong social cohesion; this type of social organization is predominantly found in the continental "tundra", the northerly "boreal" forests and sub-tropical regions having an arid climate. The use period of their dwellings is several months or seasons.

The semi-nomadic society represents a transitional phase in the evolutionary process. It could therefore equally be described as semi-sedentary, especially since many tribes have abodes in a fixed locality to which they return from time to time. Similarly, it is only natural that common traits should exist between nomadic and semi-nomadic dwelling forms. For example, it is not infrequent that members of these tribal communities use temporary shelters during the migratory period of the year.

People who are primarily dependent on cultivated plants and domesticated animals for food are, of course, bound to more limited areas than are nomadic hunters and food gatherers. This dependency upon adequate land for subsistence, coupled with a direct control over cultivated plants and domesticated animals, develops an explicit notion of property absent in previously mentioned social organizations. However, this notion of property or ownership of land still has the simple characteristic of communal property in contrast to that of personal or individual ownership prevalent in an industrialized society. Depending on the degree to which a group of semi-sedentary people relies upon the collective labour of its members, property becomes either community or family oriented and the extent of necessary group participation is inversely proportionate to the effectiveness of productivity. Thus, the greater the level of productivity of farming and herding is, the fewer the members who are required to contribute; the prerequisite of family holdings is a productivity by which each family can, through its own labour, produce enough food for its own needs.

60

The diversity of environmental factors and the level of productivity prevalent bring about a great variety of building types. Nevertheless, the dwellings of the semi-nomads or semi-sendentary people have certain shared characteristics. To begin with, these people often utilize distinct types of dwellings, one substantial type for their sedentary period of life and another more temporary structure for the duration of their migratory life. The first type, namely the more substantial dwelling of the two, naturally varies in magnitude according to the size of the conjugal family, the extended family or the "clan" that occupies the single or compound dwelling. In contrast to the village like setting of their substantial dwellings, the shelters used during the migratory period are scattered and are designed to accommodate smaller social units only.

Since a part of their economy is based upon cultivation, semi-nomads must have some form of granary or storage buildings adjacent to their dwellings. When their social cohesion is very strong, it is not unusual for them to have communal storehouses as well.

NAVAHO HOGAN AND RAMADA

The living quarters of the Navaho may serve as a good example for the two seasonal prototypes of substantial and temporary family-size dwellings used alternatively by their inhabitants; the first type is the HOGAN and the second the RAMADA.

The Navaho live in the arid regions of the south-west United States, an area that is characterized by high mesas, large sand and gravel plains, deep canyons and rugged mountains. In spite of considerable rainfall, this region is arid because most of the precipitation falls in torrential rains that erode the land rather than making it fertile. In summer, the Navaho move to the highlands which are more favourable for farming, to cultivate their crops, whereas during fall, winter and spring, they live in the lowlands with their livestock.

The basic social unit of the Navaho is the extended family; this group consists mainly of the parents and their married daughters and their families. Two or more extended families have an established right over a territory cultivated collectively. A larger but non-local sub-group fo the tribe is the clan of the mother.

The traditional and more substantial dwelling of the Navaho is the hogan, a mud-covered log hut with a doorway facing the east, from where all good spirits come, according to their beliefs. The hogan is a low one-room structure inhabited by a single family; several hogans are grouped closely together to house the individual units of the extended family. The older type of hogan consists of three forked poles locked together at the top with other poles leaning on them, the whole structure covered with earth. The more usual type has a circular plan with upright forked poles supporting a log deck and sloping walls all covered in turn with tamped earth. These dome-shaped huts do not have windows and the smoke of the open fire escapes through a smoke hole in the roof. A blanket is often used for a door.

Navaho Hogan

The construction of the conventional hogan commences with the digging of a two-foot deep circular pit. Four forked posts are then erected near the edge of the pit, roughly equidistant from each other; these posts are usually very crooked since only scrubby short trees are found in this arid region. Two long poles are laid parallel across two sets of forks to act as supporting beams for a number of lighter poles and branches spanning the two beams; still lighter branches are frequently laid on top of these at right angles to make the roof deck even stronger, not dissimilar in principle to the reinforcing rods of a two-way reinforced concrete slab. To construct the wall of the hogan, branches from local bushes are collected and stuck into the ground along the periphery of the circular pit and bent over to touch the edge of the roof. The upright branches are tied at the top to the roof structure and other branches interwoven horizontally around the frame, with a door opening left facing the east, just high enough for a man to crawl through. Finally, the whole brush framework is covered with moist desert earth scraped up in baskets after a rain. After a while the desert earth gets very hard and dry in the sun, making the walls and roof cover almost like plaster. Indeed, the hogan is very comfortable both during the day and at night, since the diurnal extremes of temperature prevalent in the region are evened out by the lag in heat loss of the thick layer of mud covering.

1.

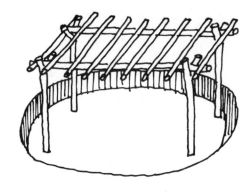

2.

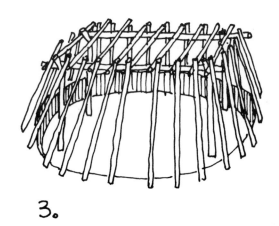

3.

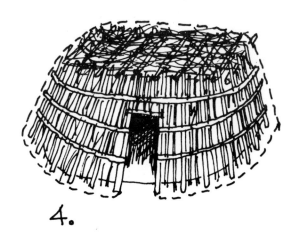

4.

Navaho Hogan

after R. Underhill

The summer homes of the Navaho are the ramadas. Essentially, a ramada consists only of four upright forked posts supporting a flat roof of poles and brush. Its sides are open and only seldom do the inhabitants erect a pole and brush wall on the windward side. The ramada is also used in many parts of Latin America and is little more than a sunshade.

House building, well digging, fencing and other major endeavours are usually communal activities. Men do most of the field work, women keep the dwellings and tend the children, while the children and the aged are expected to look after the livestock.

Navaho Hogan

NUER KRAAL

A second example of seasonal dwelling prototypes are those inhabited by the Nuer, a Nilotic tribe living in Sudan.

The Nuer are essentially a pastoral people, but though they grow a few crops to augment their food supply, cultivation of the soil is a secondary activity and is considered degrading, whereas stock breeding is viewed with great pride. Milk is the staple food of the Nuer; it is drunk fresh, eaten mixed with millet as a porridge, allowed to sour or churned into cheese. During the dry season, when cows are running dry, the Nuer bleed their cattle from a small cut in a neck vein; they boil the blood until it is thick or let it coagulate, after which it is roasted and eaten. Cattle are only butchered and eaten when they are injured or too old for breeding.

During the rainy season, the Nuer live on the upper plateaus of southern Sudan in village-like settlements containing from fifty to several hundred persons. Here they breed cattle and cultivate small plots. At the end of the rainy season, after the ground becomes arid, the Nuer set fire to the grass to prepare new pastures for the following season, and set off to camp near streams or rivers for the next six months. Frequent migrations during the dry season are necessary to ensure adequate pasture for their livestock.

The village community of the Nuer is called the CIENG, a word which may be translated as *home*, while the cattle camps used in the drought season are known as WEC, a word meaning *camp*. Grazing and the use of all vegetation are common rights of all members of a community.

The substantial dwellings of the village community form a KRAAL consisting of a cluster of round mud huts and cattle byres constructed of wattle and daub. Each kraal is inhabited by the minimum economic unit, namely a single conjugal family or an extended or joint family composed of a patriarch and several sons and their families. Building and repairs generally take place early in the dry season when there is plenty of straw for thatching. Fences are erected between the byres along the sides of the kraal and around huts to control the movements of cattle in the rainy season.

Nuer Dwelling

A single round hut is occupied by a wife and her children and, at times by her husband. In a polygamous residential family group with joint family occupancy, the homestead consists naturally of several round huts in addition to the byre. This group is called the GOL, a word synonymous with *hearth*. Each gol herds its own cattle and performs its domestic tasks independently.

In the dry season, during the period of camp living, the Nuer families sleep in the beehive huts and men often sleep in the open behind the windscreens. These temporary shelters are erected in a few hours and are sited a few yards from water, generally in a semi-circle or in line with their backs to the prevailing wind. These shelters are constructed of grass and millet stems. The stems are packed upright in a narrow semi-circular trench to make a windscreen; huts are formed from these windscreens by binding the tops together and plastering them with dung on the outside.

During the period of camp living, the economic acivities of the Nuer are communal, their cattle are herded together and milked at the same time, but during the rainy season economic activities of the homesteads are individualized.

MASAI BOMA

Seasonal dwellings are also inhabited by the Masai tribes living on the rolling plains of Kenya and Tanzania.

Small family groups of Masai travel with the seasons and herd cattle in a cyclical fashion by following the rain and the availability of pasture. Skill in cattle breeding has made the Masai tribes among the wealthiest of Africa's pastoralists. By the age of six, boys have already begun to learn how to handle cattle and at ten or twelve take care of the family herd. Later on, young men become herders and warriors protecting the large tribal herds from wild animals. A MORAN, as a warrior is called, is not allowed to work, drink alcohol, smoke or eat vegetable food. He must live on milk and blood alone, the staple food of the Masai. A bull is bled from his jugular vein, about a gallon a month, and a cow about a pint. Masai eat only the meat of their own cattle, sheep and goats and consequently do not hunt the wild herds of zebras, wildebeest and other animals grazing peacefully side by side with the domesticated cattle. They live in harmony with the wildlife in the natural haven of the Serengeti Park.

The Masai home, called BOMA, is a circular kraal ringed with high thorn fences. Just inside and adjacent to the protective fence several huts are erected. On the right-hand side of the gate, at the entrance to the boma, stands the first or main wife's hut; the second wife builds hers on the left side, and the third on the right again. Women build their huts by forcing branches into the earth and bend these towards the centre interweaving them to form a lattice framework. The resulting structure is plastered over with cow dung and mud; to make the huts watertight, a layer of hides is often placed on them.

The huts resemble rectangular earthmounds measuring seven to ten feet in width and ten to thirteen feet in length with rounded corners; they are so

71

Masai Boma

low that one cannot stand upright inside them. The interior, lit only through a narrow door opening, is divided into three use areas. The first, near the entrance, is reserved for small domestic animals like calves, the second for children and the third for adults. Small fires, constantly burning in the huts, fill the rooms with smoke.

At night the cattle are driven into the central space of the kraal for protection against wild animals. When the dry season forces the Masai to move in search of new waterholes and better grazing grounds, or if someone dies inside the kraal, the boma is abandoned. Their goods are loaded onto donkeys to be transported to the new site and their former homes are set afire before leaving.

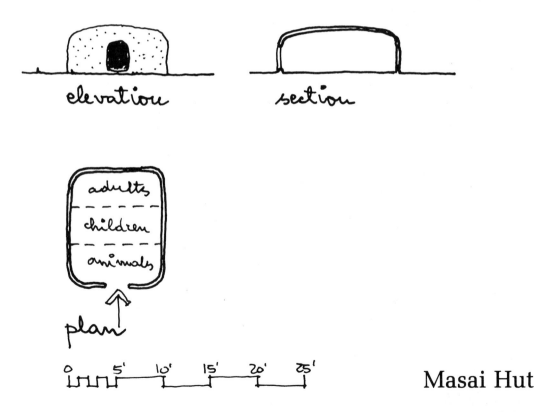

elevation   section

plan

| 0 | 5' | 10' | 15' | 20' | 25' |

Masai Hut

5

SEMI-PERMANENT DWELLINGS

The fifth stage in the evolutionary hierarchy of dwelling types consists of the huts and houses of a sedentary society. This society has a predominantly social organization known as a "folk" community subsisting mainly through land cultivation of staple crops. The members of this type of society are also often referred to as hoe-peasants; although they may use a rudimentary plow, they have not yet reached the advanced stage of agriculture in which sophisticated plows and other farm implements are used for the cultivation of fields. With the exception of irrigated plots, primitive cultivators have to leave their lands fallow for a few years after the yield of their crops decreases. In accordance with their cultivation system, effective use period of the semi-permanent dwelling varies from a few to many years.

There is no single pattern of culture or form of socio-economic organization that can be said to be an infallible characteristic of a hoe-peasant society. A wide range of physical environment, coupled with great diversity of crops, techniques of cultivation, organization of manual labour and cultural inheritance, obviously bring about many types of settlement patterns. Yet, in spite of these complex variables, we can establish some general traits pertaining to this social group and the dwellings that they build.

In contrast to the previous social groups mentioned—hunters, food gatherers, fishermen and pastoral nomads—who also resort now and then to cultivation of naturally productive areas as described earlier, the hoe-peasant deliberately cultivates through regular planting of sorted seeds, tubers or cuttings in fields that are prepared to yield staple crops. Over and above an empirical knowledge of plant life, the cultivator has to have foresight and an established routine in order to ensure a continuing supply of food. He has, for example, to store supplies not only for that period of the year when there is no produce, but also for sowing or planting of the following year's crops. The most elementary ways of tilling the land involve one or more of the following steps: clearing and burning over the plots in the dry season using digging sticks as planting implements for ridge and mound cultivation or, planting irrigated plots enclosed by embankments. The storage of cultivated food supplies allows an increased population density in a given area, complemented by a greater spot concentration of human settlement in the form of villages.

The anticipated use of a dwelling for a few years naturally imposes greater care in its construction and the resulting buildings are more durable than most nomadic shelters.

The basic dwelling forms are the cylindrical hut with the conical thatched roof, the oval house and the rectangular cabin or house with a saddle-type roof. In its simplest form, the semi-permanent dwelling has only one room which the occupants often share with small domestic animals. At the other end, we find complex clusters of huts; these dwellings are usually occupied by an extended polygamous or composite family.

Since storage facilities are required, structures serving this purpose are erected. Other ancillary buildings are not uncommon, such as pens and stables for domestic animals, as well as kitchen houses.

It is of interest to note that public buildings such as temples make their appearance at this level of social organization.

PUEBLO

An interesting and very picturesque example of a collective semi-permanent dwelling form is the American PUEBLO inhabited by the Hopi, Zuni, Acoma and other Pueblo Indian tribes living in the semi-desert plateaus of Arizona and New Mexico. Pueblos are multi-storey buildings arranged around one or more plazas; they are singular in mass, but multiple in use and meaning.

The Pueblo Indians are sedentary and peaceful people cultivating staple crops on lands which are marginal for agriculture because of limited rainfalls and growing seasons curtailed by frost. To secure adequate harvests of maize, beans, squash, gourds, tobacco and cotton, the Pueblo Indians must take advantage of the runoffs and seepages from the higher plateaus and mesas which receive more rain; moreover, they have to use drought-resistant and quick growing plant varieties suitable for deep and widely spaced planting. Even today few Indians own plows, preferring the simple wooden digging sticks, weed-cutters and hoes of pre-Columbian times. Men perform the great bulk of agricultural work, assisted by women during planting and harvesting only. Their fields are perpetually suited for cultivation since soil fertility is constantly restored by wind blown and alluvial deposition of new soil.

In pre-colonial times, the turkey and the dog were the only domesticated animals until sheep and other livestock were introduced by the colonists. In addition to farming, the Pueblos at one time did some hunting of buffalo, deer, and above all, rabbits. Women collect fruits of yucca and cacti, as well as berries and piñon nuts, especially during times of famine. However, the principal framework of Pueblo life centered—as it still does today—around agriculture.

The social organization of the Pueblo Indian is based on a matri-lineal and matri-local clan system and tribal society. The clan owns the springs, gardens and farmland; women own the home furnishings and the stored crops, while men own the livestock, tools, personal effects and religious ceremonial objects.

Pueblo Dwelling

Balance and harmony govern their view of nature and human society with men's and women's tasks complementing each other. In their communalistic society, the notion of "my room" is an incongruity and consequently impossible to express in their language.

The collective pueblo is composed of numerous rooms—sometimes hundreds —forming a homogeneous tiered structure. This closely built building mass is usually three to five storeys high with each flat-roofed and terraced upper storey on the plaza side set back from the one next lower but ending with a multi-storey perpendicular wall in the rear. The pueblo is an additive and cumulative building structure that accomodates the spatial needs of both a diminishing or increasing number of its inhabitants; in fact, the pueblo periodically changes its mass and form due to new additions as well as the demolition of dilapidated sections.

The thick walls of the pueblo are built of adobe brick or stone laid in adobe mortar; in the past, walls were frequently made of tamped mud laid in formwork. Both externally and internally, walls are plastered with clay mud; the interior is, in addition, whitewashed with fine white clay or decorated in colour.

Across the walls, peeled cedar beams about one foot in diameter are laid with small poles placed transversely and close together. Cedar bark, brushwood and grass are then placed on the poles to form support for a three- to four-inch coat of adobe. Since the main floor beams are precious building materials and are rare in an arid region, they are constantly re-used and are not trimmed to the specific length required to span the bearing walls; the excess length of a beam is allowed to penetrate beyond the face of the exterior wall and thereby creates a characteristic visual feature of the pueblo.

Traditionally, the external walls had no door openings and only a few small windows. Access to the rooms was gained through an opening in the roof through which rude ladders permitted passage; today, side doors and larger glazed windows are very common. Ladders still give access—as in the past—to

Pueblo Dwelling

the first and each successive recessed roof terrace. These ladders and the projecting ends of ladders through the roof holes are yet another unmistakable visual characteristic of the pueblo.

Each individual dwelling unit consists of a number of rooms measuring from six to eight feet in width and eight to twelve feet in depth; these are usually arranged two or three deep with the innermost room used for storage. The rooms in a suite are connected to each other by small doors.

The fireplace is usually built in a corner of the room and a hood over it carries the smoke to the chimney. In another corner, parallel with the wall, are located the slab-lined mealing bins with stone metates for grinding corn.

The extensive roof terraces are used for sitting, sleeping, winnowing grain, drying crops, and, last but not least, as viewing platforms to observe public religious ceremonies and dance performances held in the plaza below. Religion, in fact, pervades Pueblo life to such an extent that it is estimated that Pueblo men spend at least half their time engaged in religious rites performed to bring rain and abundant crops.

The secret part of religious rituals, however, is performed in the sacred rooms, or KIVAS, located in the plaza area near the base of the pueblos; traditionally, kivas are large circular sub-terranean chambers and resemble an earlier form of the Pueblo pit-house. In addition to serving as places of worship, kivas are used as council chambers, meeting rooms and workshops by the initiated men only. Kivas are entered by a ladder through an opening in the roof; they are carefully orientated with a raised platform for observers on the southern part; a fire pit and the SIPAPU, or "place of emergence", are situated on the northern part. In the Pueblo Indian's poetic mind, the kiva represents the universe; the roof and walls are the firmament, the floor is the earth. Around the walls are benches for the initiated members of the Pueblo society, and beyond these are the imaginary "cloud seats" where the gods watch ceremonies in their honour.

Pueblos are frequently built on high steep-sided mesas; in former times, these elevated sites were advantageous for purposes of defense and were also used as building sites as they were unsuited for agriculture. The building material, adobe, in conjunction with the collective building form and large mass of the pueblo results in a harmony with its natural surroundings to a degree that it is almost indistinguishable either in colour or mass from the dramatic mesa formations.

Pueblo Dwelling

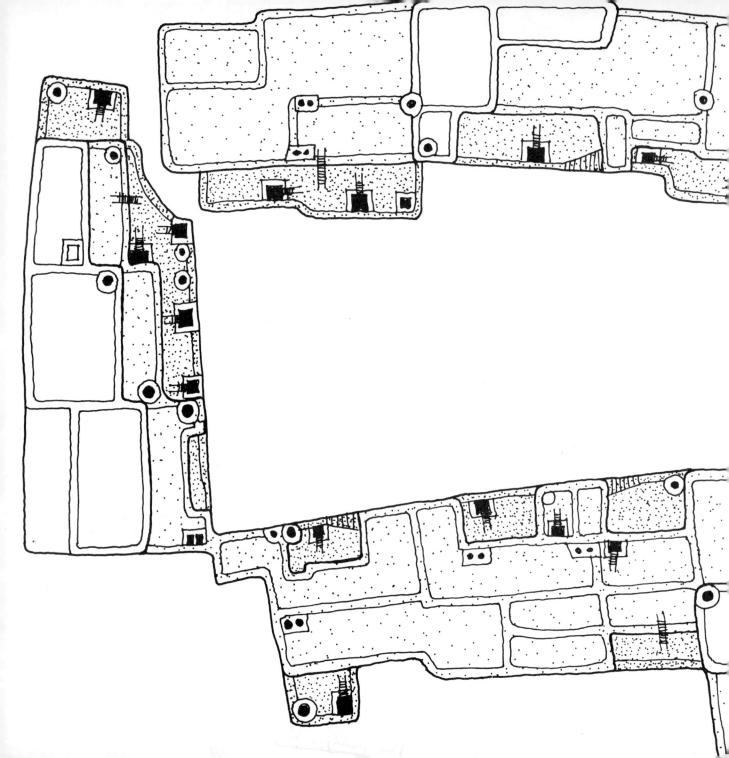

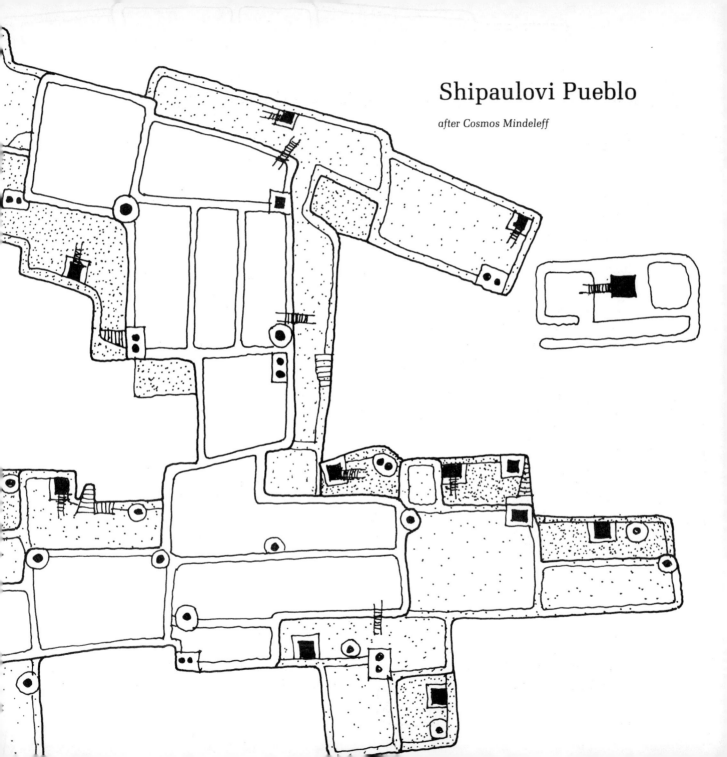

Shipaulovi Pueblo

after Cosmos Mindeleff

MASAKIN QUISAR CLUSTER DWELLING

The round hut clusters of the Masakin Quisar or Nuba people living in Sudan, in Africa, are typical examples of multi-unit semi-permanent dwellings.

The chief activity of the Masakin is the cultivation of fields of their staple food, durra, a variety of millet resembling maize. Sowing commences in April when the rainy season begins and is completed by the end of May. The fields are tended during the long growing season until November when the harvest starts. The harvest is a community endeavour and neighbours and relatives join in reaping each man's crops and then move on to another's field. Men wield knives or iron spearheads to cut the grain-bearing ears from the stalks and flail the ears of millet with flat clubs to thresh out the grain. Women clean the grain by lifting filled calabashes in the air and trickling their contents into baskets while the wind carries off the chaff; the women then transport the baskets to the granaries of their homes.

After the harvest, cattle are driven to the fields to graze on the stubble; however, cattle raising is only of secondary importance in this region of scanty grazing. Before the next sowing season, fields are burned over in preparation for spring planting.

A typical Masakin dwelling consists of five round huts constructed on stone foundations. The windowless huts, as well as the walls closing off the spaces between them, are built of adobe and are mud plastered smoothly inside and out. The huts linked by walls enclose a private family courtyard with a cooking place in its centre.

A conical grass roof covers each round hut giving it a turret shape, while a roof of loosely woven grass and boughs shades the courtyard. The main portal to the compound has the shape of a keyhole to admit a person bearing a bulky load. Each hut is lit through a small round or oval door opening with a high mud threshold and is reserved for a particular household activity. Thus, one hut is the main sleeping hut, several are storehouses and one is an animal pen for chickens, goats or pigs; the animal shelter often contains

elevation

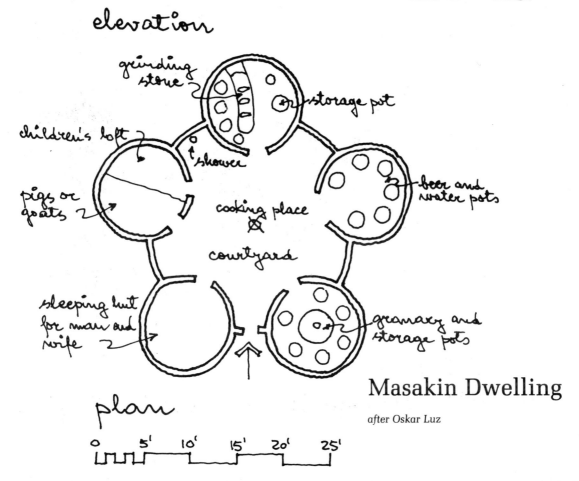

grinding stone

storage pot

children's loft

shower

pigs or goats

cooking place

beer and water pots

courtyard

sleeping hut for man and wife

granary and storage pots

plan

Masakin Dwelling

after Oskar Luz

0   5'   10'   15'   20'   25'

Masakin Quisar Cluster Dwelling

a loft reached by a separate portal at a higher level and is used as a sleeping platform for children of the family. Between two turrets of a cluster dwelling, an elementary shower is contructed consisting of a clay pot cradled on a pair of antelope horns; the bather has to reach up and tilt the water-filled pot so water can stream from a hole near the rim of the vessel.

When first married, husband and wife live with their own families until the wife becomes pregnant; at this time the Masakin start building their dwelling complex. If the husband has several wives, he must provide separate dwellings for each and must have additional fields and livestock to support each family.

AWUNA CLUSTER

Indigenous to the Upper-Volta region is the Awuna (or Fra-Fra) house, a typical example of an African round hut compound dwelling. Each dwelling unit consists of a cluster of round huts facing an enclosed central courtyard. Since each wife with her children occupies a cluster dwelling, several clusters surround the perimeter of the greater extended family compound which is also enclosed by a circular or elliptical wall centering on a cattle corral.

Each cluster dwelling of these settled, agricultural people is designed to accommodate animals such as goats, domestic hens and guinea fowl in addition to its human inhabitants. The various round huts of the cluster dwelling have assigned functions; one is invariably a sleeping room, one is a kitchen, one a storehouse. Others may be used as children's sleeping rooms, fowl house or a goat pen, according to particular needs.

The round huts and enclosing walls are constructed of mud. Most huts are roofed with thick thatches of straw on a frame structure of cut branches. The storehouse roof is usually flat and is made of mud on wooden rafters, the flat surface being used for drying corn and other farm produce. After the roofing is completed, a wood fire is kindled inside each hut to blacken the rafters, the wood frame and the thatch in order to discourage termites. The mud walls and flattened floors of the dwelling are plastered with mud mixed with cow dung and a juice extracted from the locust bean pod which hardens into a waterproof and smooth finish. None of the round huts have windows. Light enters the huts through low doorways which are only four feet high. Mud thresholds, nine inches high, are built just inside door openings to keep out the rain water. In the main sleeping hut the bedstead is molded out from the wall; a low mud wall separates a section from the kitchen to screen goats tethered to posts.

The yard has a gentle fall and is drained through a channel under the outer wall and adjacent to a screened-off washing area. Conical nesting boxes for domestic fowl are built into the enclosing yard-walls and shallow seats are molded out of the high wall enclosing the outdoor cooking area. Another section of the yard, used also for drying produce, is enclosed by a one-foot high mud wall which acts as a seat. Finally, the thatched roof of the main sleeping hut is extended outwards to give a sheltered outdoor sitting area.

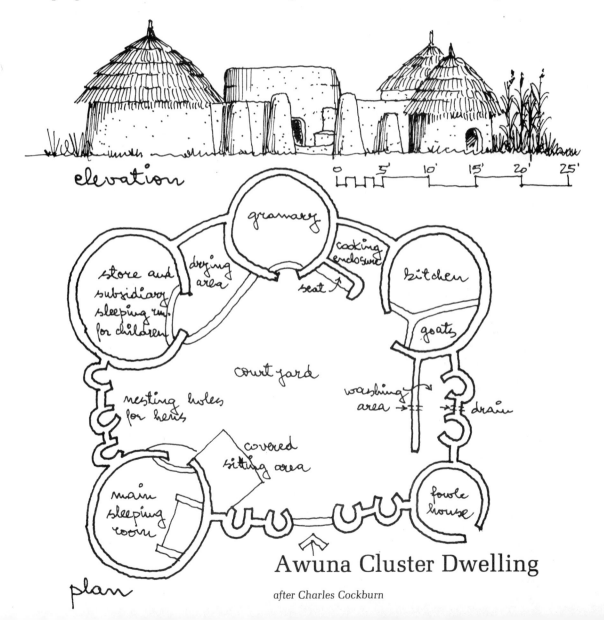

elevation

0   5'   10'   15'   20'   25'

granary

store and subsidiary sleeping rm. for children

drying area

cooking enclosure

seat

kitchen

goats

court yard

nesting holes for hens

washing area

drain

covered sitting area

main sleeping room

fowle house

Awuna Cluster Dwelling

plan

after Charles Cockburn

DOGON CLUSTER DWELLING

The Dogon people of Mali also live in a cluster-type dwelling, but in contrast to their Awuna neighbours of the Upper Volta, their huts are mostly rectangular or square in plan.

The Dogon are agriculturalists and cultivate their meagre arable land collectively. They live in compact village communities near the cliffs of the Bandiagara Plateau. There are two basic village types, namely the "plateau" type built on elevated tablelike rock outcroppings between arable fields and the "cliff-debris" type built on the steep slopes of fallen rocks along the escarpment of the Bandiagara.

The various cluster dwellings are built collectively and adjacent to each other; this collective facet of their life explains the compact nature of their communities.

Dwellings are placed around a family yard defined by the main house, granaries and secondary huts linked by stone walls. The huts and granaries rest on foundations of stones and branches; their walls are constructed of sun-dried mud bricks reinforced with bits of straw and then mud plastered.

The main house is a multi-room complex consisting of an ante-room, the family room, storage rooms and a kitchen. It is interesting to note that the kitchen section of the house has a primordial plan and is a round hut, but, like the rest of the house, is covered with a flat roof; the flat roofs are mud plastered and are supported by wooden rafters, beams and columns where needed. From the ante-room or kitchen a notched ladder gives access to the roof where the family sleeps during the hot, dry months. Beams and rafters are allowed to protrude beyond the outside face of the walls in order to act as scaffoldings when the mud walls need to be repaired.

The flat roofs of the granaries, however, are frequently covered with an additional conical straw roof. These straw roofs are assembled on the ground like

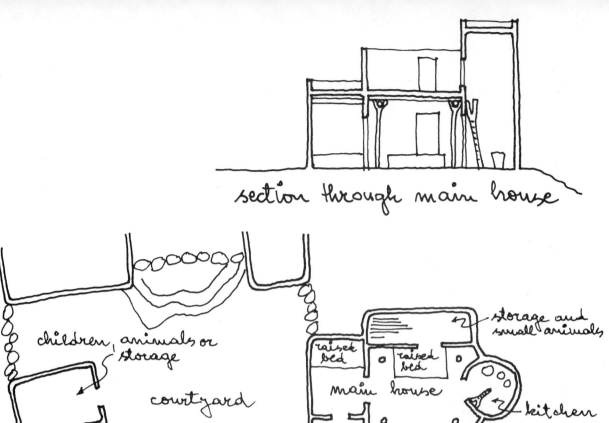

section through main house

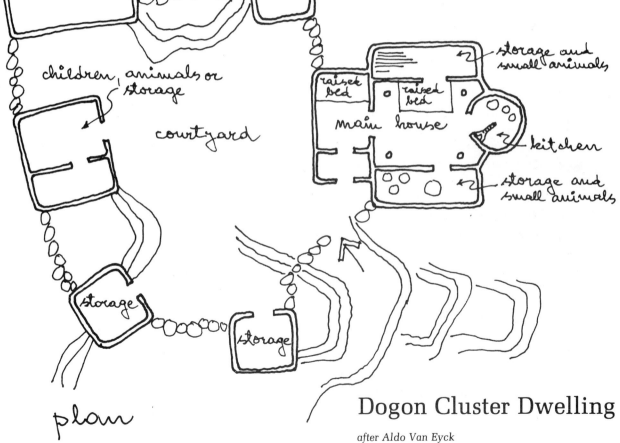

children, animals or storage

courtyard

storage and small animals

raised bed

raised bed

main house

kitchen

storage and small animals

storage

storage

plan

Dogon Cluster Dwelling

after Aldo Van Eyck

0   5'   10'   15'   20'   25'

Plateau Type Dogon Village

Cliff-debris Type Dogon Village

Dogon Dwelling

straw hats and placed on the square-based towerlike granaries. Since the conical straw roofs do not complement the square shape of the granaries, the eaves are always uneven. Each family has several granaries; some are used to store a portion of the harvest to feed the family during the dry season; others are used to store grains not only for sowing in the following season but also for supplies as insurance against crop failure. The latter granaries have wooden doors which are sealed with mud plaster and the grain inside sprinkled with ashes as protection against insect damage.

The Dogon dwelling is a good example portraying an advanced stage of the evolutionary process between the circular and the rectangular plan; moreover, it illustrates the mixed use of the single-room and multi-room structure.

MAYAN OVAL HOUSE

Another typical semi-permanent house is the Mayan oval house found in the village communities of the Yucatan peninsula in Mexico.

The Mayan people are agriculturalists living in almost self-sufficient village communities. However, when a family's arable land becomes depleted, it has to leave the village and move to another site in order to cut and burn new fields out of an overgrown wilderness that years ago may have been cultivated. At first the family retains its ties with the home village but these ties eventually vanish when a new village communitity is established in this new location.

With a small ax, a new field is cleared in autumn, the beginning of the dry season. After a few months the field is burned over and just before the rainy season commences in the late spring, maize, beans and squash are planted in small holes made with a digging stick. Following the planting of these crops, the fields are hardly cared for until harvest time in the late fall.

All members of the Mayan "folk" community are predominantly tillers and all specialized occupations, such as carpentry and storekeeping, are subordinate to farming. Their settlement is grouped around a square with a village well and a place of worship. The village consists of simple one-room homes having corn stalks or wattle and mud walls and thatched roofs. This type of house is oval shaped with a door placed in the centre of one of its broad sides.

The interiors of these homes are simply furnished with hammocks for sleeping and little wooden benches to sit on. Cooking is done in the centre of the room on a small stone hearth. The food is either boiled in a clay pot or baked on a clay griddle.

Mayan Oval House

MEXICAN JACAL

Similar to the Mayan oval house is the JACAL found in southern Mexican villages. Their inhabitants are primarily agriculturalists.

The walls of the rectangular jacal are constructed of corn stalks tied together with vines. The roof structure is also held in place by knotted twine and forms a Latin cross gabled thatched roof. There are no windows in the jacal, but the apertures between the vertical stalks allow cooling breezes to blow through the hut. A single doorway gives access to the interior of the jacal with its tamped dirt floor.

Usually the jacal is part of a compound of similar huts surrounded by a corn stalk fence. The main sleeping jacal for the parents and their young children is the largest hut in the compound. Often a second or even third jacal is built for sleeping quarters of older children. The kitchen hut is similar to the sleeping huts, but has one or more sides open towards the courtyard; moulded low adobe platforms serve as cooking hearths, and stone metates are used to grind the corn. Finally, a circular granary called CUESCOMATL is erected near the centre of the compound. The floor of the granary is elevated above the ground to protect the corn from rodents. Its supporting structure is plastered inside and out with clay to keep it dry and its conical roof is thatched to shed the rain.

The huts of the compound are detached, thus enabling their owners to burn down outworn structures and to replace them with new ones without disrupting too much their everyday life pattern.

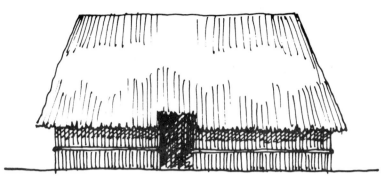

elevations

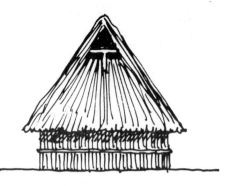

Mexican Jacal and Dwelling Compound

after Eleanor Smith Morris

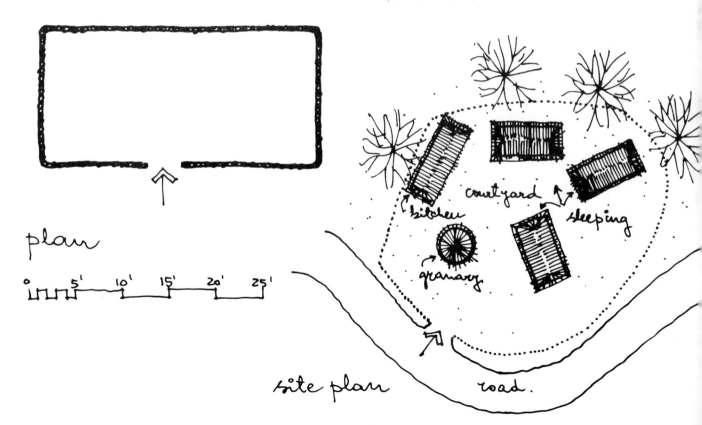

plan

0   5'   10'   15'   20'   25'

kitchen

courtyard

sleeping

granary

site plan   road.

6

PERMANENT DWELLINGS

The sixth prototype of dwelling forms reflects the advanced facets of agricultural societies that brought about the village house as well as the isolated farmstead. Dependent upon the land that they till, members of these rural societies are usually representative of an ultra-sedentary people; thus the effective use period of their home is that of a life-time or indeed several generations.

The basic unit of their social organization is the family. In accordance with the improved agricultural techniques used and the number of men required to produce food, the type of family unit in its respective society varies, in some instances being the extended or composite family while in others the conjugal or nuclear family. The social hierarchy is well established and is complemented by a political hierarchy that commences with the village, township or county and ends in nationhood.

Advanced and stabilized food production is accompanied by full-time division of labour since men not needed for food production can specialize in other endeavours. This complex way of life represents the most advanced stage in social development so far discussed.

This level of social complexity depends on surplus food production ensured by compound tools with a power source other than man, on development of storage and distribution facilities, and, finally, on a fairly well-developed transportation system. However, agriculture is at this stage of social development still a basic occupation of mankind as it provides the major source of food supplies essential to life.

The primary social consequence of the proliferation of food production, accompanied by specialized manufacture of goods and their distribution through commerce, implies a weakening of the social structure based on kinship lines and a strengthening of class ties along occupational lines as well as a differentiation of wealth. Moreover, with increased control over domesticated plants and animals, an explicit notion of property is developed by advanced agriculturalists; land becomes property explicitly and privately owned.

At this level of social development, agriculturalists permanently clear the land; they practice rotation of crops or fallowing, or fertilize the fields; their attention is directed toward the care of the field rather than to the care of individual plants.

There are two distinct types of agriculture, namely Oriental and Occidental. Agriculturalists using the Oriental practice concentrate on rice growing and use horticultural techniques such as the development of terraces, irrigation systems, diked fields, the transplantation of seedlings, the intercropping of several kinds of plants and the use of organic fertilization which ensures the permanent use of fields without rotation or fallowing. Occidental agriculturalists, on the other hand, use farming techniques such as the plowing of dry fields, the use of organic and mineral fertilization, the broadcasting of seed, the cultivating of a single crop in each field, and the rotating of crops and fallow fields.

The impact of agriculturalists on the natural landscape is very great since they permanently clear large expanses of land of their indigenous vegetation and replace them with cultivated fields. Soil impoverishment and accelerated erosion often follow in the wake of cultivation. However, this land degradation is not inevitable nor omnipresent, and consequently agricultural people can successfully live in balance with nature. Agricultural societies may appear to be living out of balance with nature, but this is often a deception; many still live essentially in ecological balance with nature but in an ecological balance of another order, namely in a modified physical environment. Due to local variations in natural endowment, land use practices and the various degrees of exchange economy factors, the population densities of sedentary agricultural societies vary from a few hundred to several thousand persons per square mile.

Since the number of variables and their complex interrelationship potentials are increased in the agricultural society and since they are not comparable to the relatively simple hoe-peasantry, it is understandable that the diverse forms of permanent dwellings are even more numerous and that a complete description of the many manifestations of their dwelling types presents a formidable task. Hence, it is necessary to resort to generalizations and merely describe the common or shared characteristics of the indigenous permanent dwelling.

There are two basic types of permanent dwellings, namely the heterogeneous and the homogeneous type. As the word implies, the heterogeneous dwelling is composed of diverse elements such as the house itself, the barn, the stable and other auxiliary buildings; the siting of these buildings can be linear, L-shaped, U-shaped or indeed quadrangular in disposition; moreover, the units of the pluri-structure may be detached or attached.

In contrast to the former type, the homogeneous dwelling embraces all activities in one structure; however, the organization of the various use areas within this mono-structure defines various sub-types depending whether a lateral, cross or vertical means of division is used to separate the dwelling from auxiliary enclosed spaces.

The permanent dwelling is invariably constructed from durable building materials; its walls are either of wood or masonry construction. The permanent character of the dwelling and occupational specialization ensure better workmanship and detailing. Doors, windows, roofs, floors and chimneys have an advanced performance standard. Interior climate control is no longer designed to the criterion of survival but to that of comfort. The dwelling is generally more spacious than previous types described; it is usually a multi-room building (although the one-room type can still be found) and the various rooms are designated for specific functions; single-purpose rooms such as bedrooms, parlour and kitchen, and multi-purpose rooms such as family rooms, are both encountered in varying degrees.

ITALIAN TRULLO

The Italian TRULLI are permanent dwellings and are the traditional building forms used by the inhabitants of the Murgia in the region of Apulia.

Cultivation is still the main occupation on the Murgia. Grapes and olives are the primary crops with wheat, beans, tomatoes and other small crops planted among the olive trees. The fields are usually small and are enclosed with thick dry stone walls. In fact, fields were made tillable through great expenditure of labour since the limestone bedrock was originally covered with but a few inches of organic soil. The preparation of a field entailed first the removal of this thin topsoil and its temporary storage; the exposed limestone bedrock was then broken up to a depth of two feet; the best stones were saved for building construction and the rest replaced with the coarse pieces on the bottom and the finest on top; red soil called bolo was brought from a nearby depression and tamped into a layer of fifteen to twenty inches on the loose limestone; finally, the stored topsoil was carefully spread over the bolo.

Very rocky areas are used as pasture land, most often for sheep. Rabbits and chickens are raised in yards and the hunting of small game is not uncommon.

The trulli are built with stones cleared from the fields, although stones quarried and excavated in the process of providing large rainwater cisterns or wine tanks beneath the dwelling are also used. Bare bedrock serves as the foundation for the trullo. The rectangular rooms are enclosed by thick stone walls hollowed in places to make alcoves and niches; the walls support a conical stone dome covered with overlapping flat stones. Similar flat stones are used for finishing the floor of the house. The tiny windows are spanned with a stone lintel while door openings are arched. The interior is invariably whitewashed and the capstone of the dome lime plastered. Rainwater is collected from the roofs in a cistern.

In a typical multi-room farmhouse, the largest dome spans the main living space; the kitchen has a large open hearth whose dome ends in a chimney;

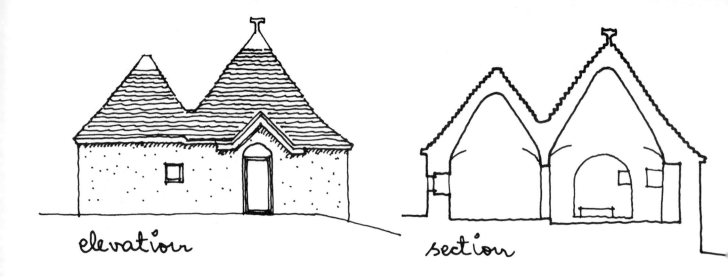

elevation

section

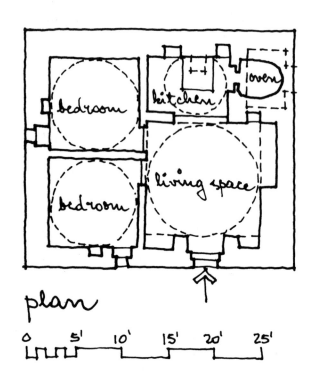

bedroom

bedroom

kitchen

oven

living space

plan

0   5'   10'   15'   20'   25'

Trullo

after Edward Allen

bread-baking ovens are either built outside the house or adjacent to the kitchen; other rooms serve as bedrooms.

During the warm seasons, the stone trulli are comfortably cool. In winter, they are cold and damp, consequently doors are kept open during the day to keep the interior dry. Many tasks such as mending and knitting are done by women who sit just outside the doorway and, as modesty demands, face the house as they work.

Entire farmsteads are built as trulli clusters, sometimes numbering up to two dozen. Hay barns have a truncated roof-cone, capped with a large and flat removable stone, with steps built into the roof to allow the farmer access to this hatch to fill the barn. Animal barns and storehouses also have the form of domed trulli and even the chicken house is a low but crude trullo.

The trullo is a rural building type of which adaptations are found in both village and city, as exemplified in large sections of Alberobello.

SLOVAKIAN FARMHOUSE

A second example of a permanent dwelling is the Slovakian farmstead, a proto-typical heterogeneous dwelling still much in evidence in the agricultural regions of Kysuce and Orava.

Slovakia is a typical mountain region; the inhabitants of the lower altitudes are engaged in farming, while those living at higher altitudes live off forestry. Shelter, degree, slope and soil conditions of the mountains coupled with frequent temperature inversions produce sharp local climatic differences that determine the selection of wheat, rye, barley or oats for cultivation or whether root crops such as sugar beets and potatoes should be grown.

Although collectivization of agriculture is professed by the present government of Slovakia, there is still considerable agricultural land cultivated by independent farmers practising small-scale mixed farming with a livestock of predominantly cattle and pigs.

The typical farmhouse of the Kysuce and Orava region is constructed of logs cut from the abundant pine woods in the mountain. The foundation is constructed of field-stone and supports the horizontally laid log walls with interlocking corners, and all joints pointed with mortar. Walls, interior posts and beams form the base of a large roof which is usually shingled. The gable ends are hipped near the ridge and at eave level in order to protect the end walls. Weather boarding covers the vertical gable section between the ridge hip and the eaves. The windows are framed by a plaster architrave and simple carvings, and decorations adorn the exterior of the house.

Usually the Slovakian dwelling is a single-storey structure except where existing slope conditions require a partially exposed cellar. This lower storey is then used as storage space, workshop or pen.

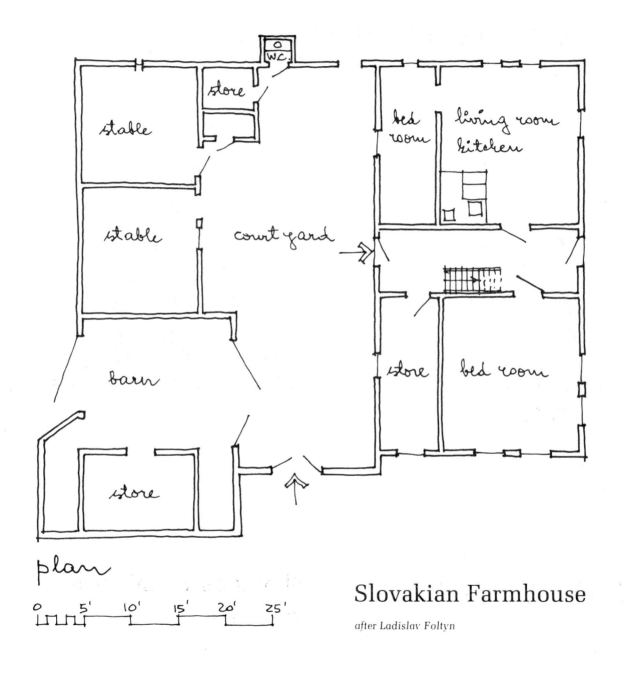

WC

store

stable

stable

court yard

barn

living room
kitchen

bed room

store

bed room

store

plan

0 5' 10' 15' 20' 25'

Slovakian Farmhouse

after Ladislav Foltyn

elevation

0   5'   10'   15'   20'   25'

Slovakian Farmhouse

after Ladislav Foltyn

The floor plan is an elongated rectangle with a transversal central vestibule dividing the house into two equal parts. From this vestibule one gains access to most rooms as well as to the loft and cellar. The principal room of this dwelling unit is a multi-purpose family room; it is used for most family activities such as cooking, eating, socializing and even sleeping. Its dominant feature is a large built-in hearth located in the innermost corner. The hearth was originally built of clay and served both as stove and oven; more recently, however, the "hearth" has been replaced by a rectangular tile stove. Wooden benches, a table, large armoires and one or two beds are the traditional furniture. A small bedroom frequently opens on to the family room. These two rooms are matched on the opposite side of the vestibule by a similar pair of rooms; they are unheated and are used for bedrooms and storage.

Wherever possible the entrance side of the farmhouse is oriented towards the south and encloses the north side of the courtyard. A parallel elongated and less substantial building embracing barn, stables and storage rooms forms the southern boundary of the yard while a roofed fence and large portal on the street side and sheds, privy, and fences on the rear complete the yard enclosure.

BERNESE FARM HOUSE

Another example of a permanent dwelling is the Bernese farmhouse. It is the indigenous dwelling of the lower-lying middle-lands of Switzerland.

The economy of the rural Bernese is mixed agricultural-pastoral; their primary agricultural crops are wheat, barley, rye, oats and potatoes, and their pastoral economy is predominantly dairy product oriented.

A typical Bernese farmstead consists of a cluster of detached buildings. The main farmhouse is the dominant structure and is surrounded by smaller secondary buildings such as the STÖCKLI (the home reserved by parents for their use on handing the farm to their heirs), the SPEICHER (the lavishly decorated granary), wood shed, pig-sty, barn and bake house.

The main multi-functional building contains under one roof the family dwelling, the stables, the hay-loft reached by a ramp, storerooms and the threshing floor. The two-storey dwelling, located at the front, is separated from the stables by the threshing floor. On the ground floor of the dwelling is found the living room and bedroom or less formal living room, both lit from the gable end. Behind these principal rooms is the large kitchen stretching from side to side and followed by two other rooms used as bedrooms and storage. Identical rooms to the first floor plan are used as bedrooms or storage on the upper level with access from a balcony reached through a steep exterior staircase.

The main entrance to the dwelling leads into the large kitchen; from here one gains access to the two pairs of rooms situated alongside the kitchen. Each set of rooms shares a *Kachelofen*, an elaborate ceramic tile oven stoked from the kitchen.

The living room is a quiet room where the family has its meals, the farmer reads and the women spin. One corner of the living room is reserved for the dining table with built-in benches against the wall. The father occupies the head of the table flanked on his right by his sons and on his left by his wife and daughters; the children take their places according to their age. Work-hands and maids sit at the foot of the table.

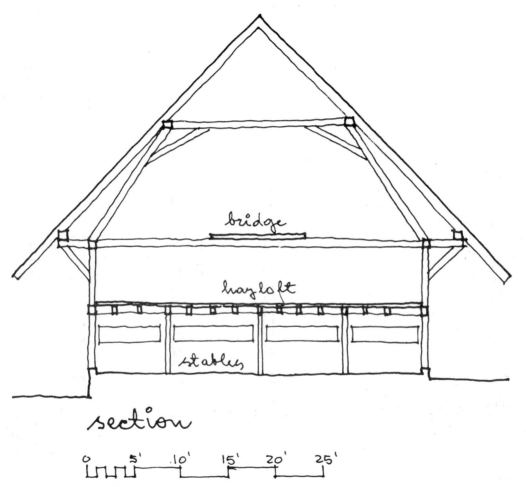

bridge

hayloft

stables

section

0   5'   10'   15'   20'   25'

Bernese Middle-land
Farmhouse

after Adrian Atkinson

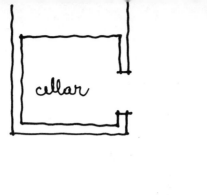

cellar

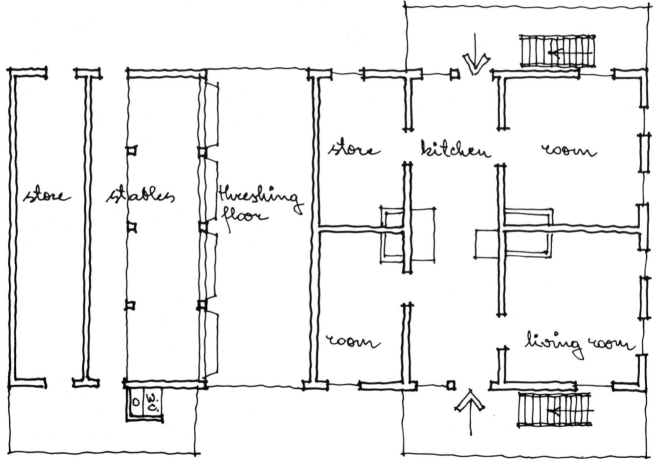

store stables threshing floor W.C. store kitchen room room living room

ground floor plan

0   5'   10'   15'   20'   25'

Bernese Middle-land
Farmhouse

after Adrian Atkinson

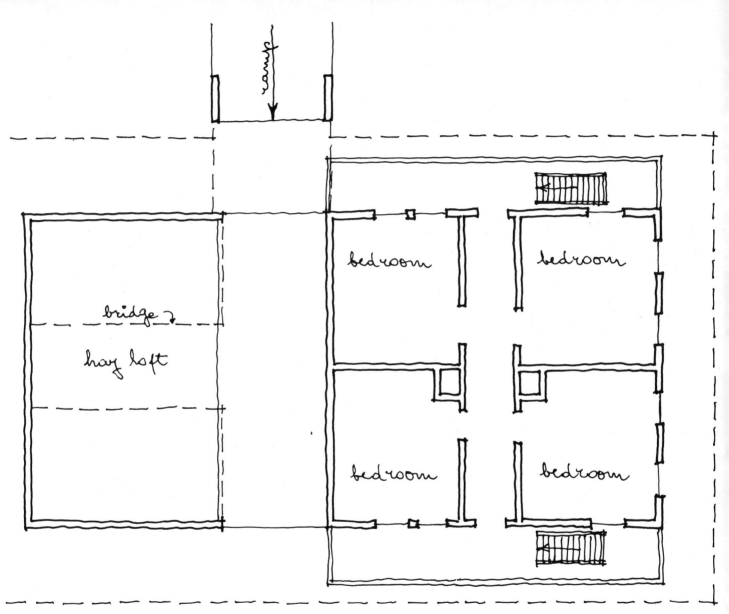

ramp

bridge →

hay loft

bedroom

bedroom

bedroom

bedroom

first floor plan

0   5'   10'   15'   20'   25'

Bernese Middle-land
Farmhouse

after Adrian Atkinson

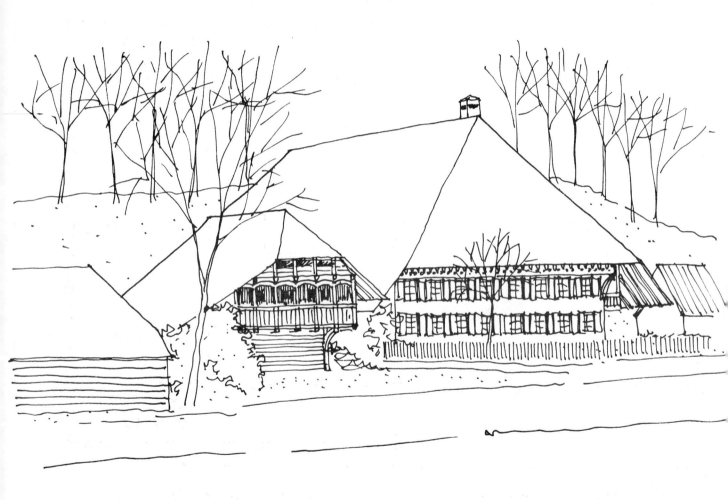

Bernese Farmhouse with Granary

The corner nearest the head of the table is called *Herrgottswinkel* or altar-corner; a cross or painting of the Holy Family is placed here.

The farmhouse has stone foundations topped with a huge ring-beam. The walls, of post-and-beam construction, support the large roof structure with its ridge-poles and close centered rafters. Overhanging eaves protect the balconies and walls. The craftsmanship displayed in the Bernese farmhouse is very advanced and reflects great concern for aesthetic considerations.

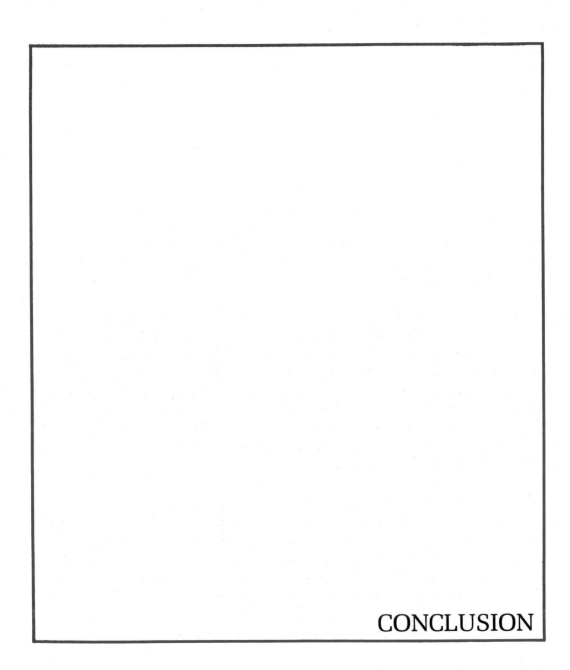

CONCLUSION

Many insights into the development of architectural form can be formed from this study of contemporary indigenous housing. Indeed, even the History of Architecture appears in a different light since it becomes evident that "time" is not the only or the most important criterion for judging architectural development. Certainly time is a factor, but only one factor among many others. Anthropogeographic and socio-economic factors have at least equal relevance to architectural development. Such notions lead to the view that time is a relative factor and consequently this study ends where Ancient Egyptian, Babylonian and Minoan Architecture begins in terms of cultural criteria. It must be admitted that Egyptian pyramids and temples, although several thousand years old, were architectural responses to cultural needs of an advanced agricultural society which incidentally had already given birth to urban communities.

In amazing contrast to the history of ancient civilizations, it is still possible today to study at first hand Stone Age cultures that chronologically speaking should have pre-dated Egyptian culture by thousands of years. Only very recently a band-type of Stone Age society was discovered in the Philippines, the Tassaday, which had had no previous contact with civilization. Though admittedly, it will not be long before all existing Stone Age cultures disappear due to acculturation and become mere distant memories; even today, quite unjustifiably, the Stone Age is dealt with in most History of Architecture courses as a mythicized period of the distant past.

If one applies knowledge acquired from the study of contemporary Stone Age cultures to view prehistoric ones, it is difficult to accept the notion that man was originally a cave dweller. For example, although the Kalahari Desert has many caves suited for shelter, the Bushmen seldom use them for that purpose; with the exception of the Tassaday, one does not find evidence of other existing band-type societies living in caves. Food-gathering nomads are constantly on the move and the notion of sedentary cave living is inconsistent with their activity; a sedentary life-style belongs to a more advanced society. Indeed,

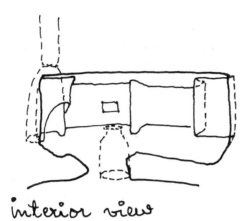

interior view

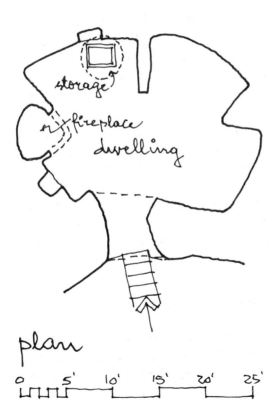

storage

fireplace

dwelling

plan

0   5'   10'   15'   20'   25'

Italian Cave Dwelling
Massafra, Apulia

after Edward Allen

caves are frequently inhabited by contemporary people, but in most instances their inhabitants are either pastoralists, agriculturalists or urban dwellers, and thus several stages removed from a primitive hunting and food-gathering society.

One cannot deny the existence of evidence found in some caves pointing to the fact that they were inhabited by prehistoric man. But, it is not improbable that prehistoric man often used caves temporarily and even repeatedly on their seasonal trek in pursuit of game. Caves may have been alternates to ephemeral dwellings; because of their very nature, beehive huts do not leave evidence for posterity to contemplate.

Yet another interesting idea is derived from the study of indigenous housing and relates to the notion that the circular floor plan pre-dates the rectangular shape of indigenous shelters. Inherently, the circular or horseshoelike floor plan represents the simplest form of shelter. The concave is womblike and maternal; it is harbourlike, inviting and sheltering; it is a "container" enclosed by a continuous line roughly equi-distant from its centre; it has no corners because it is conceptually a corner, though round. Finally, the concave circular plan is an "intuitive" form in sharp contrast to the rectangle or square both of which are rationally or intellectually devised forms.

The circular plan also appears frequently in the indigenous architecture of advanced societies which predominantly use the more sophisticated rectangular form as floor plans of their buildings. Invariably, however, the presence of such circular plans can be linked to primordial dwelling forms that survived, for example, as places of worship like the traditional kiva of the Pueblos or, in another instance, the kitchen round hut of the Dogon dwelling.

The circular plan has two intrinsic characteristics restricting its maximal development. Firstly, it has a definite threshold to enlargement or expansion due to structural reasons; with the increase of area, the diameter increases proportionately and a limit is soon reached where spanning the structure

section

plan

0   5'   10'   15'   20'   25'

Cameroon Cluster Dwelling

after Douglas Fraser

Labels within plan: younger son, ash hut, barn, goat shed, chief's hut, son's 2nd wife, son's calf, chief's quarters, 1st wife, son's 1st wife, storage, storage, storage, chief's ox, wife's hut, kitchen, kitchen, kitchen becomes a formidable task in societies in which only simple tools and building materials are used. In contrast, the expansion of the rectangle is limited in width but not in length.

Secondly, circular floor plans are hard to adapt to cumulative or additive growth. The adaptability to expansion of the rectangle or square, on the other hand, is much simpler and more economical both in terms of building materials and efficient space utilization.

The hierarchy of dwelling prototypes is complemented by a sequence of plan shapes commencing with the circle, developing into the oval, followed then by the elongated rectangle with rounded corners and finally ending with the angular rectangle or square.

Obviously, a hierarchy can also be distinguished in terms of building construction complexity. The most simple shelter, such as the beehive hut, has a space enclosure that is both roof and wall; there is no differentiation between them. The next stage is the separation of walls and roofs, first using the same building material such as wood and thatch for both, but then different materials such as adobe for walls and thatch for roofs. Similarly, the door in the most simple dwelling is in addition a window and chimney; gradually the various functions are delegated to single-purpose building elements, namely access to the door, lighting to the window and smoke exhaust to the chimney. The word window, in fact, derived from "wind eye" which meant an opening in the roof, a combination of smoke hole and open skylight.

An interesting conclusion derived from this study is related to the hierarchy of building size. Advanced socio-economic development is not complemented by gradual increase of dwelling structures. The malocas and bohios of the Amazon Valley Indians are much larger buildings than most dwellings of more advanced societies. Similarly, the pueblos are both larger and more complex in spatial organization than homesteads of agriculturalists using improved farming methods.

elevation

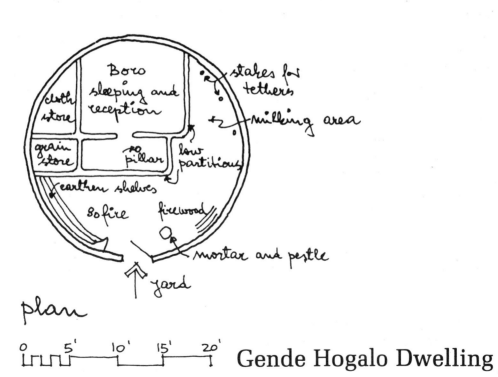

Boro sleeping and reception

cloth store

grain store

stakes for tethers

milking area

pillar

low partitions

earthen shelves

so fire

firewood

mortar and pestle

yard

plan

0   5'   10'   15'   20'

Gende Hogalo Dwelling

The explanation for this seemingly disparate hierarchical development is attributable primarily to the socio-economic structure of their respective societies. We must realize that the size of a viable economic and social unit in terms of number of people required for subsistence cultivation is inversely proportionate to their degree of technical advancement. In other words, the more primitive the method of cultivation, the greater the number of workers required to till the land in order to ensure enough harvest for subsistence. Collectivism and communalism at this level are essential life-styles for survival, features that are reflected in the construction of large communal dwellings.

It stands to reason that with the gradual improvement of agricultural methods, the viable economic unit decreases from a tribe to that of a composite or extended family which is followed by the conjugal family, first with many children and later with few. Naturally, the dwelling size complements these changes in the number of inhabitants and gradually becomes smaller until the stage is reached where additional improvements to agricultural methods replace the "survival criterion" with a "comfort criterion". At this turning point, the size and complexity of the dwelling becomes a function of increased affluence.

GLOSSARY

APA — Campsite of the BaMbuti Pygmy.

BOHIO — Communal dwelling of the Motilone Indians.

BOMA — Masai homestead ringed with thorn fences.

CIENG — Village community of the Nuer.

CUESCOMATL — Circular granary of a Mexican homestead.

FITO — Sapling used for the skeleton of BaMbuti Pygmy hut.

GOL — A group of Nuer homesteads.

HOGAN — Mud-covered log hut of the Navaho Indians.

IGLOO — Snow dwelling of the Inuit (Eskimo).

JACAL — Mexican oval house.

KAO — Hut of the unmarried young Bushmen.

KIVA — Sacred sub-terranean chambers of the Pueblo Indians.

KRAAL — Cluster of round huts and cattle byres enclosed by a fence.

LADANG — Forest clearing for short-term cultivation in Indonesia.

MALOCA — Communal dwellings of the Erigbaagtsa Indians.

MILPA — Forest clearing for short-term cultivation in Latin America.

MORAN — Masai warrior and cattle herder.

PUEBLO — Communal dwelling structure of Indian tribes living in the semi-desert plateaus of Arizona and New Mexico.

RAMADA — Summer shelter of the Navaho Indians.

SIPAPU — "place of emergence" of the kiva

SKERM — Beehive hut of the African Bushmen.

SPEICHER — Bernese granary.

STÖCKLI — Home reserved by Bernese parents for their use on handing the farm to their heir.

TRULLO — Domed stone shelter indigenous to Apulia, Italy.

WEC — Cattle camps of the Nuer.

WERF — Campsite of the African Bushmen.

YURT — Portable dwelling of Mongolian nomadic tribes.

BIBLIOGRAPHY

Abercrombie, Thomas J. "Saudi Arabia, Beyond the Sands of Mecca". *National Geographic*, Vol. 129, No. 1, (January 1966), 1-53.
_____. "Venezuela Builds on Oil". *National Geographic*, Vol. 123, No. 3, (March 1963), 344-87.

Allen, Edward. *Stone Shelters*. Cambridge, Mass., The MIT Press, 1969.

Amsler, T.; Herrmann, D.; Lohrer, K.; Pedolin, B.; and Weber, V. *Corippo*. Stuttgart, Alexander Koch, GmbH, 1959.

Anderson, Cardwell Ross. "Primitive Shelter". *AIA Journal*, (October 1961), 33-39.
_____. "Primitive Shelter". *AIA Journal*, (November 1961), 46-54.

Atkinson, Adrian. "Bernese Middle Land Farmhouses". *Shelter and Society*, New York, Frederick A. Praeger, 1969.

Bemis, Albert Farwell, and Burchard, John, II. *The Evolving House*, Vol. I, Cambridge, Mass., The Technology Press, 1933.

Cockburn, Charles. "Fra-Fra House: Damongo, Ghana". *Architectural Design*, XXXII, (June 1962), 299-300.

de Lauwe, Paul Chombart. *Famille et Habitation I*. Sciences Humaines et Conceptions de l'Habitation, Paris, Centre National de la Recherche Scientifique, 1959.

Dolfus, Jean. *Les Aspects de l'Architecture Populaire dans le Monde*. Paris, Editions Albert Morancé, 1954.

Englebert, Victor. "The Danakil: Nomads of Ethiopia's Wasteland". *National Geographic*, Vol. 137, No. 2, (February 1970), 186-211.

Evans, Clifford, and Meggers, Betty J. "The Wai-Wai of Guiana". *Indians of the Americas*, Washington, The National Geographic Society, 1955.

Evans-Pritchard, E.E. *The Nuer*. Oxford, Clarendon Press, 1940.

Fitch, James Marston, and Branch, Daniel P. "Primitive Architecture and Climate". *Scientific American*, (December 1960), 134-44.

Foltyn, Ladislav. *Volsbaukunst in der Slowakei*. Praha, Artia, 1960.

Fraser, Douglas. *Village Planning in the Primitive World*. New York, George Braziller, 1968.

Frazer, John E. "Kuwait". *National Geographic*, Vol. 135, No. 5, (May 1969), 636-67.

Grzimek, Bernhard and Michael. *Serengeti Shall Not Die*. London, Hamish Hamilton, 1959.

Ionescu, Grigore. *Architectura Populara Romineasca*. Bucuresti, Editura Tehnica, 1957.

Jorgensen, Vetle. "Traditionelle husformer i arabiske oaser". *Arkitekten*, No. 21, 1965.

Kenney, Nathaniel T. "Ethiopian Adventure". *National Geographic*, Vol. 127, No. 4, (April 1965).

Konecny, Lada Patricia. *Slovak Vernacular Architecture*, Graduate student essay, 1970, School of Architecture, McGill University, Montreal.

Larousse. *Encyclopedia of World Geography*. London, Paul Hamlyn, 1969.

Luz, Oskar. "Proud Primitives, the Nuba People". *National Geographic*, Vol. 130, No. 5, (May 1966).

MacLeish, Kenneth. "Stone Age Cavemen of Mindanao". *National Geographic*, Vol. 142, No. 2, (August 1972), 218-49.

Morgan, Lewis H. *Houses and House-life of the American Aborigines*. Chicago, Phoenix Books, The University of Chicago Press, 1965.

Morris, Eleanor Smith. "Tepoztlan: Native Genius in Town Planning". *Architect's Year Book, XI*, London, Elek Books, 1965.

Rapoport, Amos. *House Form and Culture*. Englewood Cliffs, New Jersey, Prentice-Hall, Inc., 1969.

_____. "The Pueblo and the Hogan". *Shelter and Society*, New York, Frederick A. Praeger, 1969.

Sahlins, Marshall D., *Tribesmen*, Englewood Cliffs, New Jersey, Prentice-Hall, Inc., 1968.

Schoenauer, Norbert. "The Inuit Igloo". *Asterisk*, No. 3, Student Publication of the School of Architecture, McGill University, (March 1965).

Schreider, Helen and Frank, "Journey Into the Great Rift". *National Geographic*, Vol. 128, No. 2, (August 1965), 254-90.

Schultz, Harald, "Indians of the Amazon Darkness". *National Geographic*, Vol. 125, No. 5, (May 1964), 737-58.

_____. "The Waura, Brazilian Indians of the Hidden Xingu". *National Geographic*, Vol. 129, No. 1, (January 1966), 130-52.

Schwarz, Gabriele. *Allgemeine Siedlungsgeographie*. Berlin, Walter de Gruyter & Co., 1961.

Service, Elman R. *A Profile of Primitive Culture*. New York, Harper and Brothers, 1958.

_____. *The Hunters*. Englewood Cliffs, New Jersey, Prentice-Hall, Inc., 1966.

Shapiro, Harry L. "Be It Ever So Humble". *Natural History*, (December 1944), 460-73.

_____. "There's No Place Like Home". *Natural History*, (January 1945), 24-38.

Thomas, Elizabeth Marshall. "Bushmen of the Kalahari", *National Geographic*, Vol. 123, No. 6, (June 1963).

_____. *The Harmless People*, Harmondsworth, England, Penguin Books Ltd., 1959.

Tschopik, Harry. *Indians of North America*. Science Guide No. 136, Man and Nature Publications, New York, The American Museum of Natural History, 1958.

Turnbull, Colin M. *The Forest People*. New York, Simon and Schuster, 1961.

Underhill, Ruth. *The People of the Crimson Evening*. Washington, U.S. Department of the Interior, Bureau of Indian Affairs, 1951.

Van Eyck, Aldo. "Architecture of the Dogon". *Architectural Forum*, Vol. 115, (Sept. 1961), 116-21, 186.

Volckers, Otto. *So wohnen die Völker der Erde*. Donauworth (Germany), Verlag Cassianeum, 1949.

Wagner, Philip. *The Human Use of the Earth*. London, The Free Press of Glencoe, 1960.

Watson, Richard A. and Watson, Patty Jo. *Man and Nature*. New York, Harcourt, Brace and World, Inc., 1969.

Wolf, Eric R. *Peasants*. Englewood Cliffs, New Jersey, Prentice-Hall, Inc., 1966.

DATE DUE

78			
JUL 6 '82			
SEP 14 '82			
JAN 25 '83			
OCT 4 '88			
OCT 5 1997			
AUG 27 2001			
OCT 12 2004			
OCT 13 2004			

392.36
Sch6

SCHOENAUER
Introduction to contemporary indigenous
housing